After COVID

After COVID

Living Together Beyond the Pandemic

Edited by James M. Houston

REGENT COLLEGE PUBLISHING
Vancouver, British Columbia

Contents

Introduction

The Challenge of the COVID-19 Pandemic
to the Future of Our Professions

James M. Houston

The need for balance has been basic since the rise of Egyptian civilization. For while animals are instinctual, humans are reflective beings. A pictograph in a tomb dating from 1972–1929 B.C. depicts goldsmiths using a balancing scale to determine the purity of the gold being used. In the biblical book of Daniel, the king is warned: "You are weighed in the balance and found wanting." Since antiquity we have had "the gold standard" for international commerce. After the Great Depression in 1930–1931, the International Monetary Fund was established to seek and provide guidance for global financial stability. Like other later international organizations, it can only provide advice, not police how an independent country can manage its budget. But the nature of ecosystems in the natural realm is also the evidence of the necessity to provide balance for sustainability and reproduction. Despite centuries of medical progress, there remains a constantly shifting balance between the web of human life and novel infectious microorganisms.[1]

To those who do not know the history of microbial epidemics, the apocalyptic current event of COVID-19 seems unprecedented. Yet since human origins there have been epidemics. The thought that a small microbe should be able to destroy world empires has always been terrifying. Often behind inexplicable historical events, there have been microbial events. In the Psalms, that ancient book whose origins go back to the Iron Age, we have one of the earliest records of an epidemic:

> I will say of the Lord, "He is my refuge and my fortress,
> my God, in whom I trust."
> Surely He will save you from the fowler's snare
> and from the deadly pestilence . . .
> You will not fear the terror of night,
> nor the arrow that flies by day,
> nor the pestilence that stalks in the darkness,
> nor the plague that destroys at midday.
> A thousand may fall at your side,
> and ten thousand at your right side,
> But it will not come near you. (Ps. 91:2–3, 5–7)

Ancient Egyptian irrigators suffered from water infections, such as blood flukes and worms, as early as 1200 B.C. and probably earlier, before records were kept. In rice growing areas, the tsetse fly generated constant cycles of sleeping sickness. As William H. McNeill has enumerated in his fascinating book, *Plagues and*

---

1. William H. McNeill, *Plagues and People* (New York: Anchor, 1998), 70.

People, humans and domesticated animals have shared diseases: poultry (26), rats and mice (32), horses (35), pigs (42), sheep and goats (46), cattle (50), and dogs (65).[2] The methodical Chinese have kept records over the centuries of epidemics, suggestive that the invasion of the Mongolian horse riders brought epidemics of smallpox and measles with them. Chinese overseas trade across the Indian Ocean brought bubonic epidemics, with records reporting outbreaks circa 610–642 A.D. Trade involving ships travelling overseas inevitably became synonymous with rats and plague.

The early Christians were aware of such epidemics, as reported by their leaders from the second century A.D. onwards, and the compassion of the early house churches did more for the spread of Christianity than any other factor. The Stoics, like the later Buddhists, had no answer to the challenge, except that Buddhism also spread by offering consolation to the afflicted. Indeed, there was possibly a much older history of epidemics in the Indus valley hydraulic civilization than even in Egypt. And this was where Buddhism originated.

The Black Death was the most terrifying event in European history. It was first recorded in the Crimea of the Black Sea in December 1347, swept into Italy by sea the same year, accompanied the Mongols overland into Hungary in December 1348, and a year later travelled across the English Channel into the British Isles.[3] Overall, a third of the population of Europe died between 1336 and 1350. Recurrent outbreaks in the next century led to the practice of quarantining ships' crews at the major ports, first at Ragusa (1465) and then Venice (1485).

The fourteenth-century pandemic shattered the age of chivalry, with its gulf between knight and peasant, which was based on birth. It made way for the Renaissance, the new age of meritocracy,

2. McNeill, *Plagues and People*, 70.

3. McNeill, *Plagues and People*, 178.

based on the skills of individuals regardless of their birth. But the pandemic also brought a new sobriety into Western culture, which developed "the art of dying well"—*ars moriendi*. This promoted a new consciousness of the melancholic that Richard Burton explored in detail in his *Anatomy of Melancholy* in the mid-seventeenth century. As Jean Delumeau has pointed out, the arrival of the Renaissance did not bring that cheerfulness of new accomplishments that we may assume it brought.[4] Rather, it expanded human consciousness and the depth of the existential self, which the philosophers of the eighteenth century were to explore, notably Immanuel Kant, Søren Kierkegaard, and later many philosophers of the age of reason.

A century later, with the arrival of the Spanish Conquistadores in Mexico, led by Hernando Cortez, no more than six hundred men conquered the Aztec empire of Montezuma, which had numbered millions before the accompanying epidemic. It was an epidemic of smallpox, a child's disease in the West, that then occurred. Terrified that their gods had failed them, the Mexicans rapidly adopted the Catholic faith of their conquerors. Francisco Pizarro repeated the same conquest of the Inca civilization of the Andes. Smallpox began in Hispaniola in 1518, spread quickly into Mexico, and reached Peru by 1525–1526.[5]

Napoleon assembled the largest armies of France, yet both in the New World and the Old World he was defeated by epidemics. In 1804 Jean-Jacques Dessalines declared Haiti—then known as Saint Dominique—a free republic. An island the size of Massachusetts, with a population of present-day Louisiana, defeated France, a world power of twenty million, for Napoleon's army was ravaged by yellow fever. This forced Napoleon to sign the Louisiana Settle-

---

4. Jean Delumeau, *Sin and Fear: The Emergence of a Western Guilt Culture, 13th–18th Centuries*, trans. Eric Nicholson (New York: St. Martin's, 1990), 551–54.

5. Delumeau, *Sin and Fear*, 217.

ment, which eliminated the French presence from expansion into the southern United States, and whose defeat contributed to the abolition of slavery in the French Caribbean. Yellow fever combined with malaria destroyed Napoleon's plans to restore slavery. Moreover, a war in the tropics was very different from Napoleon's wars in Europe.[6] Instead of mass attacks, it was a military operation of small groups.

Disaster followed disaster for Napoleon when he then invaded Russia in 1812. He did so to recruit more soldiers in Poland to serve in his *"grand armee"* in an effort at ending Russian trade with Britain. He was now at the peak of his power, blinded by what he thought he could do. After Russia, why not then march into India? It was the same *hubris* as that of Alexander the Great, whom he cited as his example to follow.

Scorning medical advice and the need for carrying provisions, the army, careless of sanitation, befouled water and food supplies; dysentery spread rapidly. It killed those afflicted within a week, yet the soldiers kept marching crowded together. By the time the troops reached Moscow, a third of Napoleon's troops had died. In their retreat, with winter approaching, typhus then took over, for by now the troops were undernourished. The cavalry was forced to eat their own horses, and then in the madness of hunger cannibalism began also. Defeated by Russian commanders' tactics, and combined with dysentery and typhus, the greatest European army ever before assembled was almost totally wiped out.

Historians who ignore the powerful influence of pandemics deny that history repeats itself. But those who recognize the powerful changes brought about by the ongoing cycles of pandemics of diseases, recognize a spiral upward effect, also bringing changes for the good. So what can we now immediately predict? Today,

---

6. Delumeau, *Sin and Fear*, 122–39.

COVID-19 challenges all professions and their institutions, rather like "the Black Death" did.

First, we are getting to the tipping point that unless we can reduce carbon dioxide in the global atmosphere, global warming will become unstoppable. The shut-down of factories, global air flights, and other causes of excessive release of carbon dioxide have given us another chance to reduce emissions in the future. The imperative to use electric-powered vehicles has also begun.

Second, the reform of many aspects of our culture is hopefully about to begin, reform that demands collaboration, globally and personally. Such a collaborative culture is needed for global transportation and the tech revolution of the internet with its vast flow of information.

Third, if democracy is to survive, further boundaries must be established to prevent dictatorships from expanding. There is not space enough for two contrastive political systems, even while recognizing that pandemics will never cease and that poor societies will always be with us. Collaboration is vital for the future onslaught of more pandemics, world hunger, and degradation of our global environment. The Assembly of the United Nations must be strengthened, not weakened by nationalism, racism, and autocracy.

These issues are cause for this edited book, where each contributor shares his or her concerns for changes in professional leadership. We begin with Ambassador Marcel Biato's essay, "Diplomacy in Times of Pandemic." He opens by quoting Louis Pasteur: "When meditating over a disease, I never think of finding a remedy for it, but, instead, a means of preventing it."

There is no cure for microbes or for greedy, evil human beings, only prevention. Rejoicing in our expanding technological advances, we have not reckoned with the reality of the recurrence of pandemics. Instead, we breathed happily that "the war to end all wars" was over, and that the diplomatic efforts to ban the use of nuclear weapons have now succeeded. It is an illusion, just as the end of pandemic diseases is also an illusion. Rather, the end of traditional diplomacy is over, and a new approach is needed. Perhaps embassies need a medical attaché added to their diplomatic staff. Greater guidance is needed with the greater future threat of global anarchy. No one country can do it alone, nor can national rulers act autocratically. Local leadership must be unleashed to inspire local initiative.

The words of Sir Halford Mackinder, founder of the School of Geography at Oxford in 1901, have become so much more relevant: "The world is a globe, where action at one point of the earth's hemisphere is reaction at another."[7] The International Monetary Fund continues to conceive of new models of "balance," whether they be financial markets data (equity prices, bond yields, etc.), frequency of cycles, mature or emerging markets, or output (various capital rates, shortfalls, liquidity ratios). The IMF critiques the weakness of models, whether they are too data intensive in their analysis, or not intensive enough.

The authoritative handbook, *Guide to IMF Stress Testing*, is all about money. But as the wise sociologist Georg Simmel pointed out, after the First World War "money" is morally neutral, and therefore monetary assessment fails to be morally comprehensive enough.[8] This defect had already been pointed out by Karl Marx in his critique of capitalism. But his model was morally ineffective when it was applied by the Russian revolutionary leaders to crush landowner and peasant alike. For social morality requires personal ethics, not just an abstract ideology.

7. This quotation was in circulation at Hertford College, Oxford when I was Fellow and taught geography.

8. Georg Simmel, *The Philosophy of Money*, trans. Tim Bottomore and David Frisby (New York: Routledge, 2011).

So now in our new apocalyptic crisis, I have enquired from business leaders, who all favor "a mild socialism" to become more morally relational. It was an appeal made by Jacques Ellul in the 1960s, haunted by the biblical challenge, "Am I my brother's keeper?" Cain thought he was not in the slaying of Abel. Brilliantly, Ellul analyzed the dynamics of envy as the origin of human competitive creativity. For this envy created in mythopoeic imagery "the rise of the city," with all its creative expressions and consumptive needs.[9]

In 1930–1931, the king of the small semi-dependent Himalayan state of Bhutan innovated a coefficient of happiness to replace a monetary standard. As a Buddhist state, the king was expressing the teaching of Buddha to attain contentment.

In many ways, Buddhism imitates and re-expresses biblical teaching, which states in the book of Proverbs: "Honest scales and balance are from the Lord" (Prov. 16:11). As Jesus confronted the rich young ruler: "What shall it profit a man if he gain the whole world and lose or forfeit his very self?" (Lk. 9:25) And as the apostle Paul, who "had learned the secret of being content in all circumstances" (1 Tim. 4:12), exhorted Timothy, it is only "godliness with contentment which is great gain" (1 Tim. 6:6).

But self-contentment can be self-deceiving, and happiness can be paradoxical, as it has become in the Scandinavian countries, who followed Bhutan by introducing the "coefficient of happiness." But according to the Danish Think Tank Institute, Denmark has the highest divorce rate per capita in Europe, and Finland has the highest suicide rate. These contradictions suggest there is a paradox about the pursuit and attainment of happiness. Chase after a butterfly, and it will never be possessed; be quiet and composed, and it may settle on your shoulder. As Buddhists well know, happiness is obedience to the throne of appetites; unhappiness is a

9. Jacques Ellul, *The Meaning of the City*, trans. Dennis Pardee (Grand Rapids: Eerdmans, 1970).

life of longing and craving, like an alcoholic. The want becomes indefinable.

In the twelfth century, the previous hoarding and robbing economy was being replaced by one of peaceful exchange. At that transition, Bernard of Clairvaux could observe: "It is folly and extreme madness always to be longing for things that can never satisfy the heart, not even blunt the appetite; however much you have these things, you still desire what you have not yet attained; you are restlessly sighing after what is missing."[10]

In the following essays, we have invited a group of leaders to consider and suggest, if a coefficient of happiness were to be added to the customary monetary coefficient, how this would radically alter their way of practicing their profession. Pivotal to this reformation would be the prime motive of global and personal collaboration. Just as the Black Plague was followed by the Renaissance culture of meritocracy, so then this COVID pandemic has to be responded to by collaboration. For the challenge today is compounded by millions of refugees and world hunger accompanied even by plagues of grasshoppers. The growing intimacy of animals and man can only be the breeding ground of new viruses, as we have seen in tropical Africa with the Ebola epidemic. Then it was association with monkeys, and now it is with an Asian bat. What will it be next? The accumulation of viruses will also accelerate with global warming. Hopefully, conflict between nations will diminish to enable the fight against a common enemy: animal viruses.

10. As quoted in Bernard McGinn, *The Growth of Mysticism* (New York: Crossroad, 1994), 199.

1

Diplomacy in Times of Pandemic

Marcel Biato

"When meditating over a disease, I never think of finding a remedy for it, but, instead, a means of preventing it." Louis Pasteur[1]

Major cataclysms are trying and stressful events. Unforeseen and unpredictable, large-scale disasters—natural or man-made—profoundly test our limits as individuals and as communities, more so because they often bring out both the best and the worst in us. We are left to speculate, despair or hope in the face of the utterly unfathomable.

As with personal crises, collective traumas undermine the delicate sense of emotional and existential equilibrium that guides us through the run of daily life. Where and how we find this balance varies enormously across individuals, continents, cultures and religions. Words such as *happiness, self-realization* and *motivation* only begin to plumb the shades of meaning with

---

1. Address on 15 May 1884, to the École Centrale des Arts et Manufactures, Paris. In Maurice Benjamin Strauss, *Familiar Medical Quotations* (1968), 451.

which people mold their personal or collective sense of being and consciousness.

For the most part, we leave it to philosophers, theologians and other speculative personalities to delve into these existential conundrums, these slippery meanders of moral unease that most of us prefer to bypass as we go about our regular chores. Getting through the day and the next gives us the illusion that things, even if not entirely understood, are more or less in sync and therefore under control.

COVID-19, beyond the widespread pain and loss it inflicts, has thrown this passive couch-potato thinking out of whack. Being cooped up at home indefinitely in fear of the silent death that prowls the streets, we feel profoundly challenged in our ingrained life style and mental habits. The pandemic is therefore an opportunity to shake off complacency in the face of dizzying change and find shared purpose in pursuit of our individual visions of fulfillment.

Know Thy Enemy

As with most onlookers, I did not see it coming. Neither did I take the threat too seriously at first. Saturated by a 24/7 barrage of overhyped raw opinion and distracted by overblown scaremongering as well as outright "fake news," most of us were too jaded to give credence to warnings over the years that SARS, bird flu and swine fever were harbingers of worse to come.[2] Personal indifference

---

2. We should have known better. There are innumerable instances where pandemics have changed the course of history: the Cocolitztli pest brought Spanish conquistadores to Middle America in the sixteenth century killed between 5 and 15 million and opened the way for Spanish colonization; yellow fever in Haiti devastated the French army, weakening their presence in North America and leading to the Louisiana Purchase; Napoleon's retreat from Moscow was as much the work of General Pestilence as of General Winter.

quickly melted away as the evidence mounted in tandem with a collective sense of powerlessness: wildfire-like spread in infections and steep rises in hospitalization in overcrowded wards amid overworked staff. It all began to sink in, but too late to avoid the worst: preventable deaths in the tens of thousands, the threat of economic collapse and untold anguish for those left to seek closure and ponder the lessons.

Advances in medical science have given us a much firmer grasp of the biology of viruses, the dynamics of pandemics and therefore how best to avoid and contain outbreaks. Yet, in view of the generally ineffectual and bungled response to the COVID-19 outbreak worldwide, we clearly remain almost as vulnerable to pandemics as at the time of the bubonic plague centuries ago. The calamitous loss of life then was many times greater, but the haunting sense of impotence, bordering on hysteria, remains with us today.

How do we fight such a treacherous adversary? We are only just beginning to understand it. COVID-19 is a highly transmissible disease, making containment especially difficult; it targets vulnerable groups and has as-yet unclear side effects, making triage and long-term planning tricky. Even more worrisome are signs that the virus may remain incubated, in one form or another, for long periods, so that the risk is high of recurring waves of infection. More sinister, this viral attack has revealed the social "dis-ease" at the core of contemporary society. It has graphically illustrated the real cost of no longer hugging each other warmly and giving solace to the economically and spiritually needy. Social distancing measures meant to keep the menace at bay have given rise to an even crueler threat: skyrocketing domestic violence resulting from families being unexpectedly wedged together over prolonged periods. Like any new viral pandemic, COVID-19 has gripped the imagination as only a threat that is unseen, untouchable and cannot be smelled or heard can. Only when it was already upon us did we begin to understand its disconcerting impact. It is like preparing for an alien invasion from outer space, with the difference that at least the extraterrestrial invaders will be visible once they have landed on Earth!

A less far-fetched analogy is the threat of nuclear contamination, most commonly associated with an atomic explosion. Like viruses, it is an insidious hazard that mostly kills silently; it is very difficult to detect beforehand. In the aftermath of the bombing of Hiroshima and Nagasaki, the impending threat of nuclear war led to diplomatic efforts to prohibit these weapons of mass destruction. Resurgent nationalism, narrow short-term economic gain and military brinksmanship trumped far-sighted proposals to ensure the development of nuclear technology exclusively for peaceful purposes. Seventy-five years on, the doomsday scenario has so far been averted, but we are no closer to world peace. A century ago, many believed that because of its destructiveness, the First World War would be "the war to end all wars." Today, many still cling to the illusive doctrine of strategic dissuasion, whereby the destructive potential of nuclear weapons to eradicate life on Earth would miraculously give rise to prudent peace. The logic is circular and self-defeating: because we fear nuclear weapons, we have learned to live with the threat rather than abolishing it.

The nuclear illusion serves as a metaphor for the widely held belief—reinforced by the collapse of the Soviet Union—in the irreversibility of the post-war consensus on economics, trade, environment and collective security. Ever-widening circles of prosperity was to be the new normal, all the more durable because it benefited, to varying degrees, almost all countries and regions. It has taken a series of major interconnected shocks to the system over recent decades to begin to shake off this complacency.

A Brave, Uncertain New World: Coronavirus and the New Normal

The post-war consensus was already unraveling as globalization began to undergo a dramatic slowdown in recent years. Despite its obvious benefits for a vast majority, with literally billions having been lifted out of poverty, globalization is highly disruptive, having accelerated the reshuffling of the international pecking order in favor of those best adapted to a global economy in rapid flux. The most notorious example of this reversal of roles is the growing feud between the US and China, which has spilled beyond trade and technology issues into a more ominous military rift, sucking Russia and other actors into a new cycle of strategic uncertainty. This has put enormous strain on the multilateral system as a whole, to the detriment of global cooperation on pressing issues. Chauvinistic strains have been added to this cocktail, leading to open rivalry not seen since the demise of the Soviet Union. Here are being sown the seeds of a twenty-first-century resurgence of disastrous competition between great powers. Even the European Union risks falling into this temptation, given the internal bickering following the largely uncoordinated, haphazard response of individual EU members to COVID-19.[3] The roll-back in international arms control commitments and the slow pace of progress on climate change are just the most visible and discouraging signs of a growing strategic struggle for control over resources ranging from rare earth minerals and biological diversity to cutting-edge cybertechnology.

---

3. Chancellor Merkel, of Germany, has belatedly expressed regret for not having endorsed Italy's request for financial support from the European Union at the onset of a pandemic that overwhelmed local resources. A proposed multi-billion-Euro bailout for hard-pressed countries remained mired in bureaucratic in-fighting among EU governments.

But the economic reordering and the resulting political and strategic realignments do not stop there. The most disruptive impact has taken place where it was least expected. Increasingly it is within countries that the backlash has been most powerfully felt, gnawing away at political consensus and social fabric. Economic dislocation, widening income differentials and a growing sense of disenfranchisement are the hotbeds of a radicalized identity politics and resurgent nationalism, which identify in globalization the source of all modern evils. The risk of environment degradation, climate change and intensified economic rivalry are ultimately collective expressions of disenchantment that strikes at the most personal level. Ever greater connectivity in the form of global supply chains and high-speed communication has often delivered the opposite of what was promised: chronic fear, crowded loneliness, and insatiable mass consumption.

Into this whirlwind comes COVID-19.[4] The fourteenth-century bubonic plague weakened people's faith in God. Today's pandemics are feeding a widespread backlash against globalization. Evidence suggests large scale conurbations, global travel, pollution and deforestation are the Petri dish incubating these viral outbreaks.[5] Are we therefore to simply throw the baby out with the bathwater? Or will the contagion serve as a wake-up call to reform rather than discard globalization? To seek greater solidarity and concerted action in the face of world-scale challenges rather than to recoil into siege mentality? The litmus test will be our ability to act preventively and collectively to contain this pandemic and

4. As well as the empowering effect of globalized communications and transport, there is a widespread current of expert opinion that attributes the increased frequency of pandemics to deforestation, urbanization, and pollution. These threaten not only fauna and flora but also bring humans into ever closer contact with wild animals and the exotic pathogens they transmit—the feared zoonoses.

5. Interview with Frank Snowden, *Der Spiegel* 18, April 25, 2020. Snowden authored "Epidemics and Society: From Black Death to the Present."

forestall future ones. However, the international blame game already under way amid highly politicized domestic squabbles over saving lives versus preserving jobs are hardly reassuring signs. Even more disconcerting is the call for going back to "business as usual" as quickly as possible. After all, many allege, it would take centuries to reverse the environmental damage caused since the Industrial Revolution. And, even if feasible, it could only be achieved at enormous cost; witness the widespread pandemic-induced distress caused by the paralysis of most economic activities. Given this dystopian horizon, is there any chance that more effective coordination over a vast range of issues of global interest including COVID-19 is likely?

A Role for Diplomacy?

The answer may lie in the skies. Not, as in the past, by looking to the heavens for guidance and solace in the face of natural disasters but rather to admire the unprecedently pristine blue skies over our megacities as a result of the lockdown required by containment measures. This was a miracle as unique and unexpected as the wild animals roaming across major thoroughfares and the return of flora and fauna to lakes and rivers previously thought irreversibly moribund. Rather than seeing the pandemic as an unqualified menace forcing us to retreat from the hope for greater collaboration on a grand, global scale, we are challenged to see COVID-19 as an opportunity to be inspired by nature's capacity for renewal. This pandemic brings into sharp focus the fact that the technical, scientific and material wherewithal is available to prevail, so long as we do not let ourselves be side-tracked by false dilemmas and self-serving defeatism. Nature's creative resilience can inspire our own individual and communal detoxification, so as to purge the poisonous mix of prejudices and intolerance that has fed the ethical, cultural as well as social distancing that has been with us since long before the pandemic. Is there a role for diplomacy in helping us give ourselves a global, virtual hug?

The demise of traditional diplomacy has been many times forecast. Distance and time lag have ceased to be an obstacle to direct, personalized contact between global leaders and decision-makers. In this reading, diplomats have become largely obsolete, at the very best devolving into bureaucratic pen-pushers going through time-worn, formulaic motions hopelessly outdated for contemporary, high-velocity cyber-society. The failings of multilateral organizations are often presented as proof of the waning of the art of diplomacy. Yet the achievements of the normative architecture underpinning globalization remain impressive, ranging from transcontinental trade regimes to peacekeeping missions. There is no doubt ample room for improvement, as suggested by the snail's pace advance toward a general climate change agreement or the World Trade Organization's failure to close the Doha Round after almost twenty years of negotiations. Even the United Nations Security Council is increasingly sidelined from peace talks involving conflicts in which major powers have a direct stake. These shortcomings have taken a toll on the efficiency and credibility of multilateralism. Yet at the end of the day these fora do the bidding of skeptical political paymasters; in these restless and frustrating times, it is up to globally minded diplomats to show the way forward.

In the midst of the present pandemic, the World Health Organization (WHO) offers a revealing case study of the challenges ahead. Its mandate is limited essentially to monitoring outbreaks, not having been empowered to detect, investigate or apply overarching measures to deal with major regional or global pandemics.[6]

---

6. During the Ebola outbreak that same year, the WHO was forced to rely on Doctors Without Borders, which is a private NGO with doctors on the ground. In 2002 at the height of the AIDS threat, UNAIDS was set up to pool the resources

This is a far cry from providing a platform for integrated planning and implementation of anything resembling a global health strategy. Yet, as COVID-19 has shown, given the unpredictability of outbreaks, more effective multilateral collaboration is essential to avoid panicky unilateral closing of borders, black markets for medical supplies, as well as uncoordinated lockdowns. Even as the present outbreak advances, at both the national and international levels, we are still scrambling to put in place a clearinghouse system that avoids hoarding and speculation, allowing urgently required hospital equipment and personnel to be shuttled according to need and not just financial clout.[7]

We have seen this drama play out before. In 2015, at the height of the Ebola outbreak, Bill Gates warned that the world was unequipped to deal with pandemics. His call for a more integrated global strategy fell on deaf ears, once SARS, MERS and Ebola had all been relatively easily contained and, more important, within their continents and regions of origin.[8] This laid-back reaction is derivative of widespread distrust in sprawling international institutions often seen as being driven by opaque interests and hidden agendas. Effective diplomatic machinery has been crucial to enhancing the performance and accountability of the likes of the WHO in the way it does business and allocates resources. Long-term planning and budgeting, for example, help deal with the temptation on the part of major benefactors, both public and

---

of eleven international organizations, including the WHO, as well the Global Fund, which invests over US$ 4 billion a year in the treatment of diseases such as tuberculosis and malaria.

7. UNICEF, in the same vein, co-leads the Diagnostics Consortium to negotiate pricing and procure molecular diagnostic tests for COVID-19 on behalf of countries and partners. In this way exploitation of emergency needs for facemasks, ventilators, and life-saving hospital equipment for private as well as political profit is avoided.

8. Snowden, interview in *Der Spiegel.*

private, to favor voluntary, ear-marked contributions that skew what should be global, supranational priorities. Partly as a result, the WHO successfully helped coordinate the Coronavirus Global Response International Pledging Event hosted by the European Union and partners to raise €7.5 billion in initial funding for the global response to COVID-19. It will help funnel private and public funding to support development and universal deployment of diagnostics, treatments and vaccines.

The WHO's enduring travails point to the recurring reluctance of governments to allocate clear-cut mandates enabling multilateral actors to do their work autonomously and efficiently. Yet even on matters that national governments guard jealously, there are hopeful precedents. The International Atomic Energy Agency (IAEA) is a case in point. As with other multilateral watchdogs, it has at its disposal a permanent staff of inspectors to oversee nuclear materials in the hands of governments. These officials are empowered to visit and inspect what are necessarily security-sensitive installations in over 180 countries.[9] In light of the very real risk that COVID-19 might become a permanent fixture on the pandemic horizon and a global security threat, why not establish a corps of epidemiological experts, including medical attaches, to monitor and cooperate worldwide to prevent and contain future pandemics when necessary?[10]

Such ambitious goals cannot be achieved without enhanced national awareness and a realignment of global public opinion. Greater access to facts and information alone however is not

---

9. It is important to recognize that the Agency distinguishes in its treatment of nuclear power states, i.e., that have nuclear arms and non-nuclear states, that do not possess them. This notwithstanding, it does provide a basis to justify some degree of national limitation and mandatory international coordination in global security matters.

10. Rubens Ricupero, former UNCTAD Secretary General. Interview in *Estado de São Paulo,* May 8, 2020.

enough. The very same internet that brings us into contact with different cultures and peoples is easily distorted by narrowly minded interest groups, their prejudices magnified by high-speed search engines that encourage invective and herd mentality. Here public diplomacy can exert a unique influence in disarming spirits. Through a variety of fora and initiatives bringing together experts, national authorities and laypeople, the groundwork can be laid to build confidence and like-minded coalitions to influence decision-makers. Sharply focused information-gathering campaigns can foster the kind of informed debate so often missing in what passes for analysis on the internet. After all, technology, like money, is at the service of the highest bidder.

Reaching out to all segments of global society is critical to raising not only awareness but also funds.[11] As with all major catastrophes, those hardest hit tend to be the poorest and most vulnerable. Success against the pandemic will never be complete as long as some are left behind and the virus is allowed to return through the backdoor. Multilateral fora, such as the Bretton Woods institutions, as well as the G20 and BRICS Summits, can be enlisted in the effort to make financial resources available to those most in need.[12] Strong and credible institutional support also helps attract private sector partnerships—via the Global Fund,[13]

11. The Bill & Melinda Gates Foundation, for example, is the second largest contributor to the World Trade Organization.

12. Recently G20 leaders agreed to allow the temporarily suspension of foreign debt repayments on the part of countries particularly impacted by the pandemic. The BRICS Development Bank will in turn provide US$ 1 billion to India to fight COVID-19.

13. The Global Fund to Fight AIDS, Tuberculosis and Malaria is an international financing and partnership organization that aims to "attract, leverage and invest additional resources to end the epidemics of HIV/AIDS, tuberculosis and malaria to support attainment of the Sustainable Development Goals established by the United Nations." According to Peter Sands, its Execu-

for example—enabling pro-bono, pragmatic solutions to help low-income countries enhance their ability to fight COVID-19. Multilateral institutions can directly or via NGOs help organize and develop appropriate measures, especially when precarious local conditions hinder implementation.[14]

New Tools for New Times

The enhanced role for diplomacy outlined above is not a passing fad but a necessary component of the wider answer required in the face of an undercurrent toward greater anarchy in global governance. This is the driver behind the partial reversal in globalization underway. The widespread adoption of far-flung supply chains and decentralized decision-making processes enabled by cyber-technology has had a widespread leveling effect on the exercise of all forms of authority and power. Both have become increasingly diffuse, domestically and globally. The "unipolar moment" inherited at the end of the Cold War has morphed into what might be described as an entropic world. The post-war architecture that previously kept parochial interests of major players in balance and those of supporting actors in check has been significantly weakened. For better or worse, today no major country or coalition has the economic, technological or moral clout to unilaterally impose any given direction or trend to the flow of international affairs. In the midst of such fragmentation, according to one analysis, we

---

tive Director, "We are facing an unprecedented global health emergency and only a global response can fight a global disease like COVID-19. To defeat COVID-19, every country's capacity to prevent, detect and respond to infectious diseases must be reinforced. We must unite to fight" (https://reliefweb.int/report/world/coronavirus-global-response-international-pledging-event).

14. Some of the issues to address include ensuring social distancing when people live in crowded shanty towns and ensuring adequate sanitary conditions when the local population has difficulty accessing clean water.

are quickly moving toward a nonpolar world marked by increased unpredictability. In this reading, the defining component of power projection is no longer fundamentally constructive in the sense of establishing some modicum of regional stability or global architecture, no matter that it was often skewed to particular interests. Rather, power is becoming a matter of "ability to disrupt, block, disable, veto, and destroy than . . . the ability to construct, enable, repair, and build."[15] In other words, we are building a relativistic, almost postmodern Tower of Babel where no communications system, no matter how technologically advanced, can hope to bridge the gulf between a multiplicity of competing voices and divergent perspectives. A dystopic reality emerges in which all goals, no matter their source or origin, are equally valid. Consensus becomes highly conditional and circumscribed, and therefore to be achieved at best incrementally. In a nutshell, a world of conflicting narratives where confidence building and credibility are at a premium.

If this tendency to increased dispersal takes hold, diplomacy must improvise and adapt to ever more complex and cumbersome problem-solving conditions. In lieu of grandiose all-encompassing schemes, the focus will be on modest, piecemeal, step-by-step advances, often at the regional or technical sphere so as to ensure all interested parties are on board. The more decentralized power and authority become, the more room there is for bottom-up solutions and schemes. Once there are no universally accepted arbiters, only by disentangling issues one by one will it be possible to avoid getting bogged down in a morass of contradictory perceptions and sensibilities. This leaves ample room for bottom-up experimentation, where knowledgeable diplomats are on their own, thrashing out solutions that bring together differing outlooks to

15. Drezner, Krebs, and Schweller, "The End of Grand Strategy: America Must Think Small," *Foreign Affairs*, May/June 2020.

identify commonalities, isolate differences, test options and forge consensus.

For business in general and multilateral organizations operating worldwide more particularly, this means devolution of decision-making to those closer to the ground. Instead of trying to steer from above, leaders must endeavor to inspire and unleash local initiative. This requires diplomatic skills to listen to and encourage homegrown expertise rather than trying to second guess policy on the basis of a masterplan concocted by technocrats and political operators working out of air-conditioned head offices.

It is hard to overestimate the impact of direct interaction and face-to-face contact in developing the reciprocal understanding and respect which is the touchstone of any meaningful and ultimately successful negotiation exercise—or human relationship, for that matter.[16] This implies being able to read and interpret the dynamics within a room where conflicting interests and divergent perceptions are arrayed. Reconciling adversaries normally has little to do with conjuring up clever phraseology or brilliant solutions that magically dissolve longstanding disagreement. Rather it requires hammering out minimal common denominators around which each side is willing to make incremental concessions because they have come to appreciate—if not agree with—their contenders. Principals will then meet in showy theatrical ceremonies to put the finishing touches on what has been agreed to behind the stage.[17]

16. This is achieved through unexpected channels and procedures. As part of the US's endeavor to develop a working relationship with the rising Chinese leadership, Jim Hiskey was sent to China to teach Chinese diplomats to play golf in the early 1970s. As a result of Hiskey's testimony, a general came to Christ, whereby he later refused to put down the youth rioting in Tiananmen Square in Beijing in 1989. He died under house arrest, but as a Christian.

17. I can offer my own testimony in this regard. From 1994 I was a junior member of the Brazilian delegation involved in bringing to an end a border dis-

By its very nature, COVID-19, which threatens to be with us in one form or another for the predictable future, is speeding up innovation and the search for flexible alternatives in many aspects of daily life, including diplomacy. The fallout from this pandemic offers a unique chance to test new technologies and adapt them to diplomacy's strengths and requirements. At-a-distance activities such as video conferencing will never totally replace pats on the back, eye-to-eye contact, the give-and-take of corridor consultations and backroom negotiations that are the bread-and-butter of diplomacy. However, bringing in labor-saving innovations to reduce cost overheads has been on the cards for years, a tendency which COVID-19 will only accelerate. The present requirement for social distancing is already bringing livestream equipment allowing virtual presence or conferencing,[18] as well as online cameras and digital tamper-proof seals adopted in monitoring activities, as in the case of the IAEA's worldwide inspections regime for nuclear facilities.

The pressure to adapt will be reinforced by growing environmental concerns. Measures to reduce carbon dioxide emissions have gained prominence in the debate over the pandemic, in so far as COVID-19 has been, rightly or wrongly, linked to ecological degradation and, by association, to climate change. More flexible,

---

pute between Peru and Ecuador that has roiled South American relations for over a century and erupted in two wars. No hotline, fax machine, or mobile phone will ever replace the painstaking shuttle diplomacy and one-on-one negotiations over four long years that brought about this victory for regional peace and security.

18. The IAEA, in collaboration with the Food and Agriculture Administration (FAO), has provided guidance on COVID-19 detection to laboratory professionals worldwide, helping to identify the virus following WHO recommendations. To this end, the IAEA conducts webinars to help health care providers around the world to adjust their detection equipment to cope with the pandemic so that they can continue to deliver their services while protecting patients, staff, and the public.

innovative modalities for conferencing will reduce the need for physical presence and therefore reduce both financial and environmental burdens associated with international travel and hosting events. Some changes, such as working from home, will become, at least partially, a permanent feature of the diplomatic landscape, encouraged by IT innovations that accommodate the new realities. Hopefully, nature's admonitions about the limits to ruthless exploitation of its resources will make us take seriously what we have always known: material wealth and individual consumption must never be an end unto themselves, distracting us from those pursuits that make us genuinely human.

The Way Ahead

The bubonic plague was a cataclysmic event killing roughly a third of Europe's population over a half century. It wrought widespread economic havoc, religious intolerance, social devastation and psychological harm that took more than a century to recover from. Yet most analysts concur that the Black Death brought about little lasting systemic change to the political or economic landscape.[19] Similarly, beyond the obvious immediate suffering and economic dislocation, reduced interdependency and an acceleration of automatization, this pandemic is unlikely to generate a wholesale reversal of globalization or profound changes in most people's lifestyle. In the short term, we will likely see less "global nomadism," that is, the intense free-flow of people, goods and factories around the world. But soon enough, the pandemic will die down, and we run the risk after a few years of reverting to the norm: forgetting the lessons of COVID-19 and just hoping for the best.

---

19. Although the demographic collapse created a labor shortage, which ended the vestiges of serfdom in Western Europe and enriched wealthy peasant families. See Cantor, *The Civilization of the Middle Ages*, 563.

We should not expect structural change to come of itself—certainly not in the wake of the finger-pointing blame game that to a large extent has botched the global response to this pandemic. Can we afford the temptation to go back to "normal" once the pandemic is over, ignoring not only the immediate implications of our unpreparedness but also the clarion call that it represents for more profound change? In fact, as with nuclear bombs, there is no undoing technological progress; there is no going back. It is for us to determine what the "new normal" looks like.

As described briefly above, multilateral diplomacy can be useful on many levels. It can help break down mental borders and mindsets that, in moments of crisis, foster a self-fulfilling insularity that encourages cultural and ideological intransigence, jingoistic nativism and other forms of self-serving prejudice. Reinvigorated diplomacy can help us recognize the common challenge facing all.

This sets the stage for a truly coordinated international effort to provide a diagnosis of what went wrong in dealing with the pandemic and how to change course. This calls for striking a difficult balance between apparently conflicting but irreplaceable goals. Effective long-term solutions require thorough investigation of causes and missed opportunities, flawed measures and procedures, but at the same time it requires not falling into the temptation of scapegoating,[20] which undermines the confidence building required for truly effective concerted action. Bypassing this stumbling block will require recognizing that among the hardest hit by the virus and, more so, by the attendant slowdown in the world economy, are the poor and vulnerable. They will demand special assistance to overcome handicaps, which if left unattended will be an incubator for new waves of mischief.

---

20. Chinese authorities are threatening to apply punitive tariffs in response to Australia's call for a thorough investigation into China's management of the outbreak in Wuhan Province.

We must then apply the lessons learned in the fight against COVID-19 to muster awareness and commitment to face up to other, interlocking challenges. Can we use the heightened understanding of the many unexpected, chilling side effects of environmental degradation to grasp the nettle of climate change? Can we reignite the waning hope in reversing the unsettling signs of a renewed nuclear arms race?

These queries beg an even more fundamental question. We had never seen the "dark side" of globalization so vividly: empowered by modern science, a virus has spread at lighting speed, inflicting death and fear around the globe. Is a downgraded version of globalization inevitable, or can we reset it so as not to have to forgo the unquestionable economic gains and political and cultural virtues of freely exchanging goods, technology and ideas? The answer to COVID-19 and to other global ills is definitely not retrenchment. Harder borders, harsher controls, stricter limits on travel and study will result in slower economic growth and, even more worrisome, reinforce ingrained biases where fake news and intolerance prosper.

As we transition to an increasingly knowledge-based society focused on innovation, diplomacy will continue to adapt. This gives us confidence that it will remain one of globalization's most trustworthy handmaidens. Technology can be a crucial enabler of—rather than an existential threat to—the noble art of the diplomat. The internet is a microcosm of globalization. The emancipatory empowerment of a well-informed citizenry inspired its creation, yet it risks becoming a haven for inward-looking, self-indulgent factionalism easily manipulated by unscrupulous minds and authoritarian forces. Public diplomacy can help galvanize the tools of the internet to its nobler purposes.

We have inured ourselves to living under the fear of nuclear war and irreversible environmental degradation. This is a grave mistake. It would be equally deadly to passively accept living under the cloud of recurring viral pandemics. Science will help with the nuts and bolts of containing and preventing future outbreaks, but as with nuclear technology it will not replace human ingenuity in acting preventively rather than simply waiting fatalistically for misfortune to befall us. It has taken a virus and the containment measures required to fight it to make us realize that collective welfare and individual well-being are not just a question of global supply chains, supercomputers and digital communication systems. Like real viral diseases, the symptoms of a deep societal malaise have been incubated in the growing urban unrest, political embitterment and institutional decay that are all on display in contemporary Western democracies.

Diplomacy can be a catalyst in molding and galvanizing the sometimes amorphous, isolated forces for renewal by providing an institutional platform to dissolve our self-imposed global social distancing. Diplomacy can transport and empower our most basic human urges to a higher level: it enables us to shake hands across geographical divides, establish cultural and ideological eye contact, and warmly embrace our common aspirations and ideals.

The brave new world rising under our feet will require redrawing established structures and rethinking long-held habits. This is socially unsettling, economically painful and emotionally wrenching. Yet it is on this global stage that diplomacy in all its facets—public and private, traditional or technological, tried-and-tested or transformative—is called to find a vibrant new voice. The alternative is to accept that Louis Pasteur was correct when he sardonically forecast that the microbe would in the end have the last word.[21]

---

21. "Messieurs, c'est les microbes qui auront le dernier mot."

2

A Europe of Good Neighbours

The Post-Pandemic European Union and the World

John Purvis

The Great War of 1914–1919 (the end of which coincided with the last major world pandemic, the Spanish flu) gave way to the errors of the Versailles Treaty, austere economics, the crash, beggar-thy-neighbour policies, the Depression, extreme nationalism, and the Second World War, in which tens of millions perished. The lesson was learnt, and the 1939–1945 conflagration was followed by a wholly more appropriate reaction—the Marshall Plan (helping Germany and Japan recover economically, democratically, and with self-respect), social programmes in health and living standards, economic growth policies, international cooperation (including the UN, UNICEF, EU, WTO, and the WHO), respect for others, decolonisation, democracy, and aid to the third world. Of course not everything was perfect. Massive poverty; the Cold War; nuclear threats; insurgencies; and racial, caste, and religious discriminations all still remained. The huge strides in technology and prosperity were often at the expense of the poorest and of the environment. Social advances in tolerance of difference were sometimes paralleled by compensating intolerances. But over- all we can afford to look back and give our efforts perhaps a B+ for providing a level of international cooperation and reciprocal consideration, which prevented a repeat of the earlier world-scale conflicts with their calamitous trail of destruction and misery.

How will we respond to the COVID-19 pandemic? Will it be the 1930s again with neighbours beggaring neighbours, national selfishness descending into squabbles about access to vaccines and therapeutic drugs, and then onto brandishing first diplomatic and then much less diplomatic weapons from behind the barri- cades? Will First World selfishness condemn the Third World to unchecked disease and penury? Surely this will soon rebound on the selfish, and all their barricades will not suffice. Or will the good Samaritan emerge from lockdown? Will enlightened good neigh- bourliness see the potential for spreading the benefits of combining and cooperating in the search for medical solutions, in promoting and spreading widely the product of joint enterprise? Will positive cooperation and openness to trade and enterprise across borders help all parts of the world recover from the economic detritus of the pandemic? Will generosity by those that have toward those who have less help to resolve the scourge of want and poverty—and the inevitable resulting urge to migrate to the richer honey pots of the world? Surely we must renew and further develop the atmosphere of cooperation and reciprocal mutualisation, which emerged after 1945, if we are to provide the peace, prosperity, well-being and happiness we would wish for our successors on this all too small and fragile planet.

I lived in Hamburg in 1946 and witnessed the destruction and humiliating degradation of that place and time. My German friends and neighbours lived in one room per family, with little or no heat and minimal food, sometimes retrieved from garbage cans. Streams of refugees were daily working their way from an East that had been transfigured demographically and politically, into an already over-crowded, devastated and destitute West. Even the European victors were overburdened with debt and shortage. And yet out of this dystopian swamp came words of wisdom, which were translated into one of the world's greatest enterprises in peace, democracy and international cooperation—the European Iron and Steel Community, which developed progressively into the European Economic Community, the European Community and then the European Union. Helped on its way by the magnanimity of its generous neighbours—from across the Atlantic the Marshall Plan, "perhaps the most magnanimous act of statecraft in history." This firmly and happily harnessed Western Europe to the Atlantic area of defence, to democracy and to market-based economics. Hamburg is now reputed to be the richest city in Europe!

The European venture was originally composed of six countries: Germany, France, Italy, Belgium, Netherlands, and Luxembourg (the United Kingdom having opted out disdainfully). It quickly prospered, moving from an Iron and Steel Community pooling the basic manufactures of war with an agricultural policy designed to smooth the anticipated move of population from country to city, to a broadly based economic and increasingly political community of nations. Democracy, market economics, human rights and the rule of law in an environment of peace and mutual solidarity were underlying tenets and continued to underpin further developments. The six founding nations, despite starting from varying states of destruction and destitution, quickly pulled ahead of their neighbours economically. They might well have been excused some disdain towards their less successful neighbours, but in 1973 they admitted the UK, Ireland and Denmark to their club, and after that Greece, and then Spain and Portugal (all three of which had recently been dictatorships). Austria,

Finland and Sweden, all neutral militarily, followed in 1995, while Norway almost did but decided against in a referendum. Then, with the Berlin Wall coming down in 1989, the whole of Eastern and Central Europe emerged from behind the Iron Curtain, which they had suffered under since the late 1940s.

This presented the now prosperous and increasingly cohesive EEC with a quandary. Its Atlantic allies (USA and Canada) had a considerable shared interest in what to do about this situation—whether to embrace those certainly European countries into the European community, or to find some other, lesser way of aligning with them and tying them to the Western way of life, politics and economics. If the politics of absorbing these recent foes into the European family were enticing, the economic challenge of bringing them up to West European levels was daunting. Certainly, there were thoughts, more particularly in the UK, that bringing these newly freed countries into the union would help to loosen its bonds and slow the process toward a United States of Europe. Some of the core member states saw the same prospect but from the opposite perspective—that this enlargement would jeopardise their desire for a more integrated and unified European entity. In any event, it was decided to proceed by offering full membership in the EC (soon to be EU) to eight and then two more Eastern European countries. Thus, with Malta and Cyprus in 2004 and Croatia in 2013, the population of the European Union reached 500 million with 28 separate member states stretching from the Atlantic to the Black Sea and the Arctic to the Mediterranean. Huge transfers of investment funds from West to East ensued in a surprisingly fast process of levelling up. The expected reciprocity was a commitment to the ideals of the Union (democracy, rule of law, mutual solidarity), which was not in all cases upheld. Disconcerting cracks in the mutual reciprocal obligation began to appear.

Aside from full membership the EU embraced further neighbouring countries with different special arrangements—the

EFTA (European Free Trade Association) for Iceland, Norway, Switzerland and Liechtenstein, "neighbourhood" arrangements for Ukraine, the Balkan and Caucasus countries, and "Euromed" for economic, social and political partnerships with all those countries on the other side of the Mediterranean from Turkey to Morocco. Perhaps the most enlightened of all such arrangements is the EU-ACP (Africa, Caribbean, Pacific) Pact with more than 100 countries and more than 1 billion inhabitants, many of them erstwhile colonies of the European nations spread over the world. Not only does this involve special trade and aid arrangements but also a "Parliamentary Assembly" in which sits one parliamentarian from each ACP country and one corresponding member of the European Parliament. This institution has the role of overseeing and advising as equal partners and neighbours on the trade and aid arrangements between Europe and these far-flung developing countries, as well as promoting democracy and social development. The Cotonou Agreement, which succeeded the previous Lome Convention and relaunched the EU-ACP pact in 2000, was renewed by the participants on April 15, 2021. At each such successive relaunch there will inevitably be a readjustment to its objectives and methods, but the overriding basis must always be its well-established tradition of promoting and substantiating good neighbourliness in a changing and challenging world. This organisation and the EU's well-developed and administered aid programmes could be a significant mechanism for distributing vaccines and other successful medical treatments for the pandemic to these countries and their mostly low-income populations.

The development of more and more interlocking arrangements between countries in defined regions of the world (EU in Europe, Mercosur in South America, ASEAN in East Asia, NAFTA in North America) and worldwide under the auspices of global bodies (such as IMF, World Bank, UN agencies, GATT/WTO) defined the full flowering of globalisation. Countries were still countries, but they also acknowledged that they were citizens of the world and as such had good neighbourly obligations to make these relationships work—just as much as having access to the benefits that globalisation provided. Not only were the Adam Smith benefits of specialisation achieved, each according to its merits and its advantages (whether of climate, resources or ability), but also each had a measure of obligation to ensure the system endured and worked for the benefit of all.

One impressive example of Europe exploiting its potential by combining and cooperating has been in research. Even within its as-yet limited budget, substantial resources have been allocated to research, including medical research, at a European level. It is not just a matter of the money, which is substantial. Even more productive has been the freedom for scientists and researchers to move effortlessly across borders to work with colleagues in laboratories and research establishments anywhere in Europe, for pharmaceutical companies to operate in an open unencumbered single market of 500 million people with simplified one-stop patenting and drug approval processes. Gradually these cooperative research arrangements are being spread beyond the boundaries of Europe with benefit to all involved in terms of new medical solutions. Every now and then during the pandemic, national leaders have seemed to revert to the "me first" approach to any medical resolution. It is much more likely that success in discovering and then in distributing vaccine and drug solutions for the coronavirus will come from cooperation and sharing. And any such success must be shared widely even with those parts of the world which have not and could not have contributed to those discoveries. Their good health is also important, and not only in economic terms which diminish the pressure to migrate. It is becoming clear that the pandemic will not be resolved anywhere until it is resolved everywhere.

The imperative for an altruistic post-war European construct was founded on a generation which experienced the alternative—when selfish beggar-thy-neighbour policies, unbridled nationalistic fervour, and self-interest resulted in misery and destruction not only for others but also ultimately for the protagonists of such policies. In the best of cases, wise counsel had just in time seen the light and taken the difficult but farsighted steps to rectify the situation (the New Deal for example). In others, like the Third Reich, nationalism was taken to the extreme and ended in destruction.

Having digested the end of the East-West Cold War in the 1990s and early twenty-first century, complacency began to set in. Holidays in the sun, ever-increasing prosperity and spending money, an amazing choice of goods and food, world-wide travel and mobility, free or next-to-free first-class medical care, peace in our time—all became taken for granted, the norm, everyone's automatic birthright. At the same time the obligations, which were the other half of the equation, the costs and rules of such a civilised arrangement, were first questioned and then resented. No longer was the wider benefit enough. Instead why not take back control—and the cash! Let the others sink. After all we are big and strong. And in the short term, yes, that might seem viable. But in the longer term . . . ? And not just for *them*, but also for *us*?

This isn't to say that the mechanisms set up to provide this "globalised" society were by any means perfect. Many might have been set up with the most idealistic of purposes and intention. They might even have been near perfect in concept and even operation at the outset. But seventy years later they may have fallen prey to inertia, neglect, self-seeking, exploitation, favouritism and, yes, corruption. They should have been checked and serviced, like any automobile, over the years. Did they still serve their original purpose? Had they adapted to current needs and conditions? Were they producing the goods as originally envisaged? Some did and do, some didn't and don't. It was really up to each and all of us to ensure that the updating and revision process was carried out in small incremental steps and on a continuing and continuous basis. Did we? Probably not enough—and as a result some fell into inefficient (or worse) condition and thereby lost their validity. But simply rejecting the World Health Organisation out of hand in the middle of a pandemic, or the Paris Climate Agreement just as the world is warming up with bush fires, hurricanes, droughts and floods peppering the headlines, hardly seems the best way. They are not perfect, perhaps far from perfect, but would it not be better to work with the imperfect to make them better rather than to dismiss them out of hand? At the very least there is a global mechanism available with which to work and improve on a globally cooperative and reciprocal basis.

The European Economic Community was to an extent protected from the tendency towards inefficiency and corruption by the constant scrutiny that it came under from its member state governments, a critical media, and increasingly from its elected parliamentarians, as their power to effect things was progressively enhanced. A succession of acts and treaties responded to a call for a more democratic European Union and a parliament with real powers of scrutiny and decision making. So the parliament's role was progressively enhanced, and democratic scrutiny of actions was progressively improved, while its scope, both geographically and in areas of competence, was greatly increased. New constitutional treaties attempted to keep up with these changes, many requiring agonising birth processes, as differing national and popular concerns and interests were aligned. This was not always easy, and sometimes it seemed almost impossible. Referenda in France, Ireland, and the Netherlands were lost and then reversed. A referendum in the United Kingdom was lost and lost indeed—and this was with the perception that there had been too much pooling of interests and obligations, infringing on "sovereignty." These objections were perceived to outweigh the positive benefits—perceived, if not actually the case. The cash outlay, the welcoming of foreigners into your country (in exchange for your welcome into theirs), seemed too much to give away—for what, a time-critical supply chain for a world-class efficient motor car industry, vine ripened tomatoes all the year round in the supermarket, foreign caregivers for the elderly in nursing homes? Only experience will tell if the savings and any new realised benefits outweigh the losses to our previous way of life and prosperity. I very much doubt it, and the thesis of this essay is to claim that maximum cooperation across national borders, reciprocity even where one side perforce reciprocates more than the other, benefits all. Nationalistic protectionism and exclusivity only results in less prosperity, less security, less well-being and less overall happiness.

At the onset of the COVID-19 pandemic in 2020, the European Union had just lost one of its major member states (the United Kingdom). Some of the recently joined East European countries (namely Poland and Hungary) were departing manifestly from the basic precepts of EU membership such as democratic governance, independence of the judiciary, and sharing of burdens. This last was most pronounced in the area of migration and asylum seekers. In a period of great turbulence in the Middle East and parts of Africa, the pressure on the European honeypot by a stream of migrants had become overbearing. Under a completely inadequate agreement in 1990 (the Dublin Treaty), it had been stipulated that the first country of entry was responsible for dealing with any immigrants or asylum seekers arriving in the EU. With the pressure from Africa and the Middle East, this inevitably devolved all the pressure on Spain, Italy, Greece, and Malta—the first countries these migrants would reach. In the 2016 mass immigration tsunami many of these migrants managed to break away towards Northern Europe. One or two countries (notably Germany and Sweden) were prepared to accept generously and courageously a large share but looked to other member states to help share the burden—as did Spain, Italy, Greece, and Malta with the continuing stream of immigrants they were also receiving on the front line. This proved impossible for most of the other member states to accept, and draw-bridges were raised. This withdrawal behind old dismantled frontiers even threatened the much-prized Schengen agreement, which provided for borderless travel across those member states of the EU and EFTA (notably excluding the UK and Ireland). Even so, this supposed threat of overwhelming immigration was very effectively conscripted by the VOTE LEAVE Campaign in the UK. This anti-migrant fever appeared also across the Atlantic and became a mantra of the nationalists in the US as well. The good Samaritan was found to be sadly missing in our increasingly self-centred and selfish societies.

As in many parts of the world, the pandemic also had a massive economic impact on Europe, on areas and sectors especially dependant on globalised trading arrangements and freedom to travel. Not only were markets closed off and consumers locked down to their non-spending homes, but just-in-time supply chains, which were the basis of their efficient, robotised and user-price-friendly production, were broken. Workforces were self-isolated and furloughed, travel was massively disrupted, profits and wages foregone, taxes not paid, loans not repaid, businesses closed for good or at least for the duration. Massive fiscal subventions by national governments were mobilised to mitigate the immediate hardships—but what about the future recovery? Europe faced a major economic challenge, and this was of particular importance for what was now a common currency area: the Eurozone. No longer could individual countries devalue or just float their currencies. This was now in the hands of the European Central Bank (ECB) in Frankfurt—far from the workshops and parliaments of Lisbon or Ljubljana. Fiscal levers were still in the hands of individual member states, but the pandemic had hurt some countries much worse than others, and those self-same countries were the ones suffering most from the aftermath of the 2008–2009 financial crisis and the migrant rush of 2016 onwards. The earlier financial crisis had seen the ECB assist the weaker countries through their ordeal, albeit with a schoolmaster's tawse in hand. The ECB had committed to do "all that's needed" to protect the common currency through its new crisis. It provided massive financial support to the most hard-pressed countries, but necessarily, being a bank and monetary authority, as loans repayable in due course. Vital help indeed, but intimidating debts piled up. This time, again that commitment was made. But monetary support was now known to be insufficient. Fiscal support was essential as well. Thankfully, for the first time the EU's Executive or Commission has been authorised to borrow huge amounts and apply these to recovery focused expenditure. One of the traditionally conservative, strict disciplinarians, Germany, has allowed that such aid should be provided by the Union's "treasury" in the form of grants and not as repayable loans. This issue of mutual support and solidarity across the European Union is to be a major test of good neighbourliness and indeed *the* test as to whether the European Union is still a Union or just a collection of friendly middle-sized states located in one of the older and historically more cultured (but quarrelsome) continents. This may be a near existential issue for the European Union, but also the world would suffer immeasurably if this prime exemplar of deep neighbourly cooperation were to refuse the jump into full-blown, finanically mutualised solidarity in such a time of dire economic crisis.

The history of the European Union and its development has advanced time and time again by facing and, after much agonising, overcoming periodical crises. It would seem that the 2020 pandemic has brought it face to face with yet another of these crises and potential turning points. It is vitally important for its future that it meets and overcomes this challenge. Ironically, the UK's withdrawal into its own splendid (and far from successful) isolation, when it would have been intractably opposed to such mutualisation of financial responsibility, has made this possible. The EU now moves into an altogether different sphere as a truly valid economic, financial, and political unit. Its credit, as the world's prime economic and financial entity with 450 million of the planet's most prosperous and productive inhabitants, will be undoubted. Its euro will truly become a world reserve resource. No longer will it be practicable to limit its budget to 1 percent of the EU's GDP, which has heretofore constrained it. With the power that the European Parliament has over that budget, the role of MEPs (Members of the European Parliament), just 750 representing 450 million persons, will be massively enhanced—and correspondingly that of national parliaments and national parliamentarians reduced. That will not be everywhere considered a happy outcome and prospect. But it will be up to the European institutions (including especially the European Parliament) to reach an accommodation with their national counterparts as to their respective roles and which preserves the localisation of decision-making ("subsidiarity") as much as possible, while providing for the benefits, which centralisation at a European level can provide.

This step on the further financial integration of Europe is only the first step in realising the precepts of good neighbourliness within Europe. There are many other areas of social, educational, economic and cultural life where the yet further development of mutually beneficial support and exchange can take place. And hopefully even more can this new phase in neighbourliness be extended beyond Europe. Not only could this be beneficial to Europe and its friends around the world, but also as an example to other major powers and groupings. Could this beneficent epidemic spread advantageously? Two areas come to mind in particular: trade and aid, both of which will be critical to the world's recovery in the pandemic's immediate aftermath. But perhaps overlaying even these must be the urgent prospect of world peace, well-being, and freedoms.

With its enhanced financial and economic powers resulting from its countries' closer integration, Europe will undoubtedly be one of the world's premier economic and trading blocs. With this visiting card it will be in a strong position to promote freer trade globally. Along with this power comes also the responsibility to assist less well-endowed countries, first to survive and recover from the pandemic and then to raise their game, to compete where they have specialised advantage, and to progress from being aid dependant to being friendly competitors and traders on equal terms. Not only does this bring them economic benefit, it also provides for national and individual self-respect. As economic standards equalise across the globe, the reason for mass movements of people diminishes. No longer will it be necessary to rescue human beings fleeing for their lives and their freedom from the waters of the Mediterranean Sea and the English Channel. If this transfers across the Atlantic, drowned fathers and sons in the Rio Grande will no longer have to disturb our consciences. Those who want to cross will cross safely and be welcome—in either direction!

If this seems to be viewing the scene through rose-tinted spectacles, we still have to consider two further very basic aspects: world peace and preservation of the planet. Can good neighbourliness starting out from one's home community, one's parish, one's county, one's country, one's continent or politico-economic unit, extend to the world at large? These seventy-five years of European peace were ensured for much of the time by military alliances, such as NATO, which held the ring at a high level of tension against equally dangerous forces, the Warsaw Pact, on the other side. With the 1989 fall of the Berlin Wall and subsequent disintegration of the Soviet Union and its acolyte states, we seemed to have reached a halcyon state of balance and peace in the world. Sadly, this has already shown signs of deterioration with the countries we were beginning to look on as friendly competitors (Russia and China in particular) becoming more like hostile and aggressive rivals. Suspicions of nefarious underhanded deeds and intentions are stalking the corridors of chancelleries and secret service bunkers. Does this need to be? They too are our neighbours, and we are theirs.

It might be too much to expect that our newfound good neighbourliness will be sufficient to bring these countries, which feel perhaps justifiably diminished and disadvantaged by our past actions and omissions, to the peace tent. But the alternative of pressuring them to yet more belligerence and defensiveness will surely only be counter-productive for all of us. It is surely worth a concerted but realistic effort to find a way of squaring this circle. Despite all our suspicions of their totalitarian and state-centred tendencies, their peoples in the end want and must be provided with a prosperous but also happy and fulfilling way of life. Material goods and benefits may appeal for a while. But with more of these also comes a desire for more education and enlightenment, more international contact and ultimately the need for more freedom. All this would be at risk without a stable state of peace. At the same time realism will demand that we be no fools. We will not be soft-soaped into giving away our own well-being for "a mess of potage"! There will even be a place for brandishing the stick and the sword—if not, hopefully, having to actually use them. Carrot and stick could be the way to be good neighbours even to those who, at first, are doubtful about being good neighbours themselves. Could the pandemic offer an opportunity for a carrot in the form of much better cooperation in the medical and public health fields? Given a renewed willingness for openness and generosity on all sides, our combined efforts could expedite the critical medical break-throughs and following economic benefits which renewal of an energetic and open trading environment would provide.

Without the perhaps utopian prospect of "beating swords into ploughshares" worldwide, it will be difficult to broach fully and positively that final challenge of saving our planet from environmental degradation, and perhaps destruction. Only when the whole world is singing the same song and acting accordingly will we truly be able to reach the mutual safe-keeping agreement which permits a way of life for its billions of inhabitants to live in harmony with what the planet can provide.

It may seem a long way from homestead to world peace and saving the planet. On the way along that transit, I see what we can achieve in Europe being one of the keys to unlocking by example that movement which will shift the world, homestead by homestead, bloc by bloc, to this long-term promise. And a good place to start will surely be in resolving the medical and economic issues of the pandemic crisis. Indeed it presents us with an unanticipated but heaven-sent opportunity to do just that. By mobilising its research capabilities to the maximum in the quest for preventative and curative medical solutions, and then by open and altruistic distribution of those beneficial results widely to all areas of the world, including the poorest, the European Union will have justified the faith placed in it as a good neighbour to all.

Although a child of war, I have been privileged to live through seventy-five years of peace in my part of Europe. Not many generations in all of history have enjoyed such a privilege. I can but hope that my grandchildren and their grandchildren can learn from the lessons of their elders and strive for that good neighbourliness which is and must be the answer for a happy, prosperous and fulfilling future. Perhaps our children will extend the benefits of that good neighbourliness more successfully than we to all parts of this world. Will this decade, with its defining pandemic experiences, be the opening to the best of better worlds? It can be.

That good Samaritan knew something—when he gave!

3

Keeping Our Eyes on the Basics

The Prospects for Renewing the Western
Alliance in a Post-Pandemic World

Alberto R. Coll

Over the four years of his administration, much debate surrounded the question of President Trump's impact on the close strategic, military and political alliance that has tied together Europe and the United States since 1945. This chapter does not intend to go over the arguments that critics have made as to whether Trump was harmful to the alliance, or, in a paradoxical way, a disruptive force that prodded some of the European allies to spend more on defense and develop new capabilities that will ultimately contribute to greater allied effectiveness. Instead, this chapter will look at the very different question of whether, over the medium and long term and quite independently of the former president's policies and his successor's stated commitment to renewing US-European ties, the alliance can flourish in a rapidly changing strategic environment. The chapter looks closely at the full range of common as well as divergent interests and values that will determine whether, on balance, the alliance can thrive and even strengthen over the next two decades. In a post-pandemic world, the same strategic and geopolitical realities visible over the last decade will reassert themselves to make the alliance of continuing fundamental importance to Western security and international stability.

This is not the first time the alliance's viability has been under question, or has seemed to face an existential crisis. Indeed, since its beginning the alliance has faced serious recurring challenges. In the 1950s, and again in the 1980s, critics often questioned whether, given the Soviets' conventional superiority, the United States would ever be willing to go to nuclear war over Europe. In the 1990s, following the end of the Cold War, others made the argument that the alliance had become obsolete. In late 2011, the Obama administration announced a "strategic pivot" towards the Asia-Pacific region,[1] followed two years later by a budget projected to shrink the US Army to its smallest size since 1941, while reducing US forces in Europe to barely 40,000.[2] In 2012, none other than that formidable doyen of the US foreign policy establishment, Richard Haas, made the argument that Europe no longer counted in world politics, the implication being that the alliance was, at best, an increasingly small appendage to America's larger global priorities.

Theory to the Rescue?

Theoretical insights from a number of disciplines may help to explain some of the long-term difficulties involved in sustaining the alliance. Long before Trump, some observers argued that

1. https://fas.org/sgp/crs/natsec/R42448.pdf.
2. https://www.csis.org/analysis/defense-cuts-sequestration-and-us-defense-budget (April 29, 2013).

free-rider theory, for example, provides a partial explanation for why European states, including such economically large powers as Germany and France, routinely spend far less on military capabilities than the United States relative to their respective GDPs. Over the course of decades, Europeans have gotten used to the idea that regardless of whether they matched US levels of military spending, the American political establishment was willing to spend considerable resources on the alliance out of its belief that it provides substantial benefits to the United States. Free-rider behavior is a common phenomenon in international relations. Indeed, the neo-realist John Mearsheimer shows the United States to have been the most conspicuous "free rider" among the great powers between 1880 and 1917, and again from 1920 until 1940.[3] During those critical periods, America massively underspent on its security while Great Britain carried much of the financial and naval burden of upholding a friendly global order.

Generational change theory, as outlined by Cambridge historian Herbert Butterfield, also yields clues to the alliance's current deterioration. In his 1958 essay on "The Role of the Generations in History," he pointed to the problem that newer generations forget, ignore, or otherwise downplay as irrelevant the insights painfully learned by the previous generation. One of his prime examples was Germany's foreign policy in the post-Bismarck era. Born in 1815 and raised in the aftermath of the horrendous thirty-year-long wars of the French Revolution and Napoleon, Bismarck was supremely attentive to the operations of the European balance of power, Prussia's need to avoid being perceived as a hegemon in the making, and the new Germany's existential requirements for a grand strategy grounded in restraint. The generations that succeeded him, however, had different perspectives grounded in their

3. John J. Mearsheimer, *The Tragedy of Great Power Politics* (New York: Norton, 2001).

increasing remoteness from the Napoleonic Wars and the chaos and uncontrollable nature of a system-wide war that afflicted Europe throughout the years 1792–1815. Bismarck's caution, obsessive attention to avoiding diplomatic isolation, and management of international perceptions of Germany—already seen by many of his younger contemporaries in the late 1880s as old fashioned if not archaic—gave way, in the span of two generations, to runaway militarism and overweening geopolitical pretensions that alarmed Germany's neighbors, especially Great Britain. Butterfield concluded his essay by observing that there is much one can learn from history's catastrophes. The problem is that the generations who live through those catastrophes and learn something from them eventually give way to new generations for whom that supposed wisdom is largely irrelevant, meaningless, or superseded by supposedly "new" realities.

Butterfield's insights are applicable to the Atlantic alliance's long-term problems. On both sides of the Atlantic, the World War II and Cold War generations have given way to people for whom the searing experiences of 1939–1989 are increasingly remote and disconnected from more pressing concerns and aspirations, be they "climate change," building more expansive welfare states, or focusing on domestic "culture wars" around issues of gender, race, and social and cultural identity. During the past thirty years, worries about China's ascendancy, disillusionment with hard power borne out of America's disastrous Middle East interventions, and various forms of isolationism have also become more widespread in the United States. In Europe, it took Russia's military intervention in Ukraine in 2014 to serve as a powerful reminder of the alliance's relevance. However, even now, alliance and security issues have to compete in Europe's public agenda with the far from unfinished consequences of the 2008 financial crisis, massive migration flows from North Africa and the Middle East, the rise of populist parties disrupting the political establishment, Brexit, and a host of environmental and social issues, which the long peace since 1945 has brought into prominence.[4]

Theory, however, does not point in any inexorable way to the alliance's ultimate demise. Many proponents of *neo-realism*, John Mearsheimer most notably among them, have suggested that there remain powerful factors keeping the Western alliance together. Chief among these is the United States' recognition that Europe, in particular its older Western core that still comprises a significant (even if declining) share of world GDP, is too valuable to abandon to the control of another power, be it Russia, a reenergized Germany, or a future China. For the sake of protecting its own long-term strategic interests, the United States has a powerful incentive to remain significantly involved.

Hegemonic stability theorists provide additional support to Mearsheimer's observation. The Atlantic alliance has created a preponderance of economic and military power marked by NATO's current boundaries. The alliance's primacy has fostered stability that, in turn, serves well the interests of all major European powers as well as the United States. For each of them, the existence of such stability is far more advantageous to their individual and collective interests than the uncertainty and instability triggered by breaking up the alliance or pulling the enormous military might of the United States out of it. However much times may have changed over the last seven decades, the alliance has a built-in, highly practical, incentive to remain in place well beyond mere inertia or sentiment.

In short, theory helps to illuminate both the long-term stresses facing the alliance, as well as the forces that keep it together. It provides insights into significant dynamics that will continue to play out within the alliance long after Trump. However, theory

---

4. The German elections of September 2021 illustrate these trends quite strikingly. See https://www.wsj.com/articles/germanys-election-results-show-young-voters-growing-influence-11633011582?page=1.

seems insufficient to indicate, by itself, whether the alliance will survive or disintegrate. For further illumination, it may be useful to turn to another set of issues: the kinds of strategic, political and economic interests that divide the alliance, as well as those that bind it together.

Divergent Interests within the Alliance

Asia-Pacific and China's Regional Ambitions

Relations with China pose a complex set of tensions and uncertainties among the allies, and is the issue most likely to roil their relations over the next decade. Since 2008, the core European economies have become more dependent on exports to non-Western countries, China foremost among them. Meanwhile, reliance on Chinese investment among European states in the periphery has surged.[5] To varying degrees, the foreign policies of European states reflect these realities. European states are far more reluctant to challenge or antagonize China than the United States.

Although Europe maintains key economic partnerships with Japan, Korea, Southeast Asia, and Australia, and 40 percent of all its trade transits through the South China Sea, it ceased to be a Pacific power a long time ago.[6] It lacks the capacity to project any kind of military power in the Pacific and has no ambitions to do so. It is thus reluctant to challenge China's unstated policy of achieving regional hegemony. The Europeans want stability in the Pacific region, but seem unconcerned, or unwilling, to take any

5. Hans Kundnani, "How Economic Dependence Could Undermine Europe's Foreign Policy Coherence," German Marshall Fund, January 2016.

6. For the argument that Europe and the United States should cooperate more closely on Asian security issues, see Ryan Hass and Alex Pascal, "Why European Partners Are Critical to US Strategy in Asia," Brookings Institution, November 2017.

action with respect to China's growing assertiveness in the region, its increasing control over the South China Sea, and the expansion of its military capabilities. These are all major regional issues that the Europeans have left to the Americans' care, and neither France, Germany, nor the United Kingdom, have been eager to antagonize Beijing and put their economic ties with China at risk over them. Up until now, this major divergence of interests between the United States and its transatlantic partners, while creating sporadic irritation, has not proved to be a defining difference in terms of damaging the alliance's cohesion. Yet, it is an open question whether this will continue to be so.

One of the key unresolved questions at the heart of the alliance is whether, in a military conflict between the United States and China over Taiwan or Japan, the Europeans would take the United States' side, thereby risking war with China, or would stay out of it altogether. Since 1951, the United States has had a mutual defense treaty with Japan, and American administrations to this day have repeatedly stated that a Chinese attack on Japan would meet a US military response. Such a conflict could escalate quickly to include American strikes on the Chinese mainland and Chinese counterattacks against US soil. As was the case on 9/11, an attack against United States territory would be sufficient cause to trigger the NATO security guarantees. However, it is not clear how Europe would respond, as European states have been deliberately vague on this issue.

This divergence of interests is equally obvious concerning Taiwan. Since 1979, and through successive administrations, the United States has formally affirmed a "one-China" policy and recognized Taiwan as part of China, while simultaneously insisting that China should not alter the status quo through force. The policy has a strong element of strategic ambiguity. On the one hand, the United States has never specified how it would respond if China uses military force to regain Taiwan; on the other, Washington has hinted on a number of occasions it might intervene militarily in such a scenario. Europe has studiously avoided being drawn into this strategic hornet's nest. Beyond issuing the usual platitudes about the need for China and Taiwan to resolve their differences peacefully, neither the alliance, nor the European Union, nor any European state has given any formal indication of how it would respond to a military conflict between the United States and China triggered by a Chinese invasion of Taiwan. As in the case of Japan, such a conflict could escalate and lead to Chinese military strikes, either conventional or nuclear, against the American heartland, posing an extremely uncomfortable dilemma for the alliance.

Unlike Europe, there has been a hardening bipartisan consensus in the United States against China since 2014. One of the few issues on which most congressional Democrats and Republicans agree is the need to toughen political, diplomatic, and military policy toward China. Obama's "Pacific pivot" evolved during the Trump years into a strategy of outright containment, with clear overtones of a new cold war between the two superpowers.[7] Much of the American establishment is far more comfortable with such a turn of events than European leaders.

The Obama-Trump policy of containing China and giving a higher priority to the Pacific has continued under the Biden administration, with its sponsorship of AUKUS, a partnership involving Australia, the United Kingdom, and Australia that will enable the latter to deploy nuclear-powered submarines in the western Pacific as a powerful deterrent against China. Unfortunately, the process through which the United States managed the creation of AUKUS reinforced European perceptions of the United States placing a higher priority on the Pacific than on Europe. Australia

---

7. See the path-breaking National Security Strategy of the United States, issued in December 2017, https://www.whitehouse.gov/wp-content/uploads/2017/12/NSS-Final-12-18-2017-0905.pdf.

cancelled a €62 billion contract with France for the purchase of French diesel submarines in order to purchase $40 billion worth of the admittedly more powerful, and farther-ranging, nuclear-powered submarines from the United States and the United Kingdom. Much worse perhaps was the wound to French pride caused by Washington's inept decision to inform Paris of the launching of the new AUKUS security partnership only a few hours before announcing it publicly. The Biden administration evidently calculated that AUKUS's value in deterring and containing China far outweighed the costs of alienating a major European ally.

This major divergence in American and European attitudes toward China, however, is not the whole story. As will be addressed later, Europe's unwillingness to challenge China's regional hegemonic ambitions does not translate into European passivity in the face of the challenges posed to European security by China's aggressive economic and investment forays into Europe. There remains a substantially large area of common interests, and the potential for a future coordinated strategy between Europe and the United States on the large questions surrounding China's ongoing quest for global economic and technological primacy.

The Middle East

Another set of divergent interests concerns the Middle East, where Washington and the European allies often do not see eye to eye.[8] This is particularly the case with Israel and Iran. Over the past three decades, American policy has tilted ever more markedly toward Israel, even as European allies have raised serious objections to this trend. Under the enormous pressures of the pro-Israel lobby, US administrations from both political parties have been

---

8. For a historical perspective on US-British rivalries over the region, see James Barr, *Lords of the Desert: Britain's Struggle with America to Dominate the Middle East* (New York: Basic Books, 2018).

part of this process. Not facing similar domestic political pressures, European governments have been freer to pursue a more even-handed approach to the Israeli-Palestinian conflict.

These differences, in turn, have shaped to some degree the allies' divergent stances on Iran. It is true that the Obama administration worked closely with Europe to secure the 2015 nuclear accord with Iran, and that much of the US national security establishment, including a number of prominent former Republican officials, supported it. Yet, many Republican political leaders fiercely opposed the deal and vowed to undo it if they won the White House, as indeed the Trump administration proceeded to do in 2017. In response to growing American pressures on Europe to join its renewed sanctions on Iran, the European Union has actively sought to encourage European companies to do business in the country. The differences over Israel and Iran should not obscure one area where the allies have cooperated closely: Afghanistan. NATO forces representing a wide range of European power have operated in the country since 2001 along with the United States, until the Biden administration unilaterally decided to end the Afghan mission in 2021. Here, too, the manner in which the administration handled the withdrawal without even a shred of consultation or regard for their interests angered the European allies and provoked anew the predictable calls from France to develop a European "strategic autonomy" independent from NATO and the United States.

Historical Precedents

These kind of inter-allied tensions are nothing new. Against heavy pressure from the United States, many European allies recognized the People's Republic of China after it came into being in 1949, something the United States did not do until 1978. Although European allies supported the American war effort in Korea, they warned the Truman administration against overreach, and pressed for an armistice as soon as practicable. The United States, in turn, did not hesitate to abandon and thoroughly humiliate France and Great Britain during the 1956 Suez Crisis. A few years later, the key European powers stood by the United States during the Cuban Missile Crisis, but they pointedly refused to join in the Vietnam War. In 1983, fresh from facing down the Soviet Union over its placement of intermediate-range nuclear missiles by agreeing to the deployment of Pershing and cruise missiles on their soil, the European allies nonetheless vigorously resisted the Reagan Administration's efforts to block construction of a gas pipeline from Siberia to Western Europe. In 1996, the Europeans were equally forceful in rebuffing the extraterritorial pretensions of the US Congress' Helms-Burton Act that targeted Europe's extensive commercial ties with Cuba.

These numerous tensions throughout its history have never succeeded in breaking up the alliance. This is because, in spite of numerous debates about whether it should expand its scope to so-called out-of-area contingencies, the alliance has kept its focus on the single strategic objective for which it was founded: Europe's defense. Even as individual allies have cooperated closely, or refrained from doing so, on various international issues, and even as the alliance has involved itself on a limited basis in missions such as Afghanistan, its focus has remained the European heartland, and this is not likely to change. It is difficult enough for NATO's European members to muster the political will and resources to maintain credible conventional deterrent forces for defensive purposes.

Common Interests Binding the Alliance

Russia and Ukraine

Russia's regional assertiveness under Vladimir Putin's leadership has quieted down much of the earlier talk about NATO's obsolescence. In late February 2014, US Defense Secretary Hagel announced the implementation of previously planned reductions in the US Army, including Europe-deployed forces, to their lowest levels since the end of World War II.[9] However, history has a tendency to confound those who studiously ignore it. That same week, a revolution broke out in Ukraine, deposing President Victor Yanukovych. In response, President Putin annexed the Crimean Peninsula a few weeks later and began to give extensive military support to pro-Russia separatists in eastern Ukraine. As Crimea again became part of Russia, the new Ukrainian government, the European Union, and the United States protested vigorously. In the space of a few weeks, NATO catapulted back into relevance. In response to the sanctions subsequently imposed by the European Union and the United States in 2014, Russia has pursued a policy intended to destabilize Ukraine and exert political and military pressure on NATO's Baltic and eastern flanks.

At issue in the ongoing power struggle between Russia and the Western allies over Ukraine is the future of a strategically situated country with over 40 million people; a large number of them admire Europe and would like to see Ukraine eventually join the European Union.[10] Allowing Ukraine to slip into a Russian sphere of influence or outright Russian domination would be harmful to the long-term economic and security interests of the European Union. It would also fortify Russian ambitions under President Putin to recover much of Russia's former preeminence in Eastern and Central Europe.

At a larger strategic level, the Ukrainian crisis is a manifestation of the strategic challenges that President Putin's Russia poses

9. https://www.csmonitor.com/World/Security-Watch/2014/0224/Pentagon-plan-to-downsize-Army-a-sign-of-US-reluctance-to-nation-build.

10. Richard Kraemer and Maia Otarashvili, "Geopolitical Implications of the Ukraine Crisis," Foreign Policy Research Institute, April 30, 2014, https://www.fpri.org/article/2014/04/geopolitical-implications-of-the-ukraine-crisis/.

for the Atlantic alliance. Russia in 2021 is not the democratic, pro-European Russia that the United States and the Europeans hoped would arise at the end of the Cold War thirty years ago. It is an increasingly authoritarian, revisionist power that sees NATO, the European Union, and the United States, not merely as competitors, but as adversaries to be weakened, intimidated, and divided whenever possible.[11] Over the past decade, Russia has upgraded its conventional military forces, and enhanced its capacity to use tactical nuclear weapons in conjunction with conventional military operations. As part of this process, it has carried out numerous military exercises testing the use of massive combined tactical nuclear and conventional forces in a war against NATO involving attacks on the Baltic States and Poland. Although President Putin does not want a direct military conflict with the alliance, he will exploit any perceived political or military weaknesses to opportunistically pursue whatever strategic gains he can find to restore Russia's Great Power status and its former regional hegemony. In a different form from the Soviet Union, Putin's Russia has emerged as the single most serious security challenge facing both the European Union and the Atlantic alliance.[12]

China's Economic and Technological Challenge

Arguably, China's quest to achieve global economic and technological primacy poses an even more serious, multi-pronged,

11. A key component of this policy has been to interfere in the political processes of the United States, Great Britain, France, and Germany through cyber warfare and support for fringe political parties. See *Assessing Russian Activities and Intentions in Recent US Elections*, Office of the Director of National Intelligence, January 6, 2017, at https://www.dni.gov/files/documents/ICA_2017_01.pdf.

12. Eric S. Edelman and Whitney Morgan McNamara, *US Strategy for Maintaining a Europe Whole and Free*, Center for Strategic and Budgetary Assessments, 2017.

and long-term challenge to the future of both Europe and the United States than Russia's geopolitical assertiveness. First, there are the economic and political offshoots of China's Belt and Road Initiative. Second, there is the "Made-in-China 2025" Plan, which has gone hand in hand with attempts to purchase or acquire controlling stakes in European and US industrial "crown jewels." Third, there is a long list of perceived widespread unfair practices by China in its trade relations and treatment of foreign investors' intellectual property rights. Fourth, there is fear that multinational Chinese companies will act to undermine the national security interests of Western countries.[13] Finally, China carries out increasingly sophisticated, extensive industrial and cyber espionage. Even though Europe and the United States are far from developing a joint strategy, their common interests in these areas provide ample scope for one.[14]

The broader background for rising anxieties about China's quest for economic and technological dominance has been a sense that the West has lost the strategic bet it made in the 1980s that it could co-opt China into the Western-led international order as a great power sharing similar values and interests.[15] Since his election to China's top leadership post in 2013, Xi Jinping has turned China into an increasingly totalitarian, repressive state,[16] while

13. "US Secures Arrest of Huawei Executive," *Wall Street Journal,* December 6, 2018.

14. Philippe Le Corre and Jonathan Pollack, *China's Global Rise: Can the EU and US Pursue a Coordinated Strategy?* Brookings Institution, October 2016.

15. Kurt M. Campbell and Ely Ratner, "The China Reckoning: How Beijing Defied American Expectations," *Foreign Affairs*, March–April 2018. "How the West Got China Wrong," *The Economist*, March 1, 2018, https://www.economist.com/.../2018/03/01/how-the-west-got-china-wrong.

16. James Kynge and Sun Yu, "China and Big Tech: Xi's Blueprint for a Digital Dictatorship," *The Financial Times*, September 6, 2021, https://www.ft.com/content/9ef38be2–9b4d-49a4-a812–97ad6d70ea6f.

establishing through military means *de facto* Chinese hegemony over the South China Sea. Under him, the Chinese Communist Party has used the most advanced social media technologies to enhance censorship over the internet,[17] surveillance over the life and daily habits of the population, stifle dissent, and cement the Party's control over all aspects of life in ways that Soviet leaders could only have dreamt of doing five decades ago. Repression in Tibet has soared, along with the importation of millions of Han peoples into the region in order to transform its ethnic, religious and social character. In restive Xinjiang, the government has placed over one million Muslims in forced detention camps.[18] In Hong Kong, China has sought to crush most dissent and tighten its political control through its promulgation of a new National Security Law. In the space of a few years, the economically booming China that was supposed to become gradually more liberal and democratic has taken a sharp turn toward an authoritarianism augmented by the latest techniques of social control. The United States and Europe have taken notice. They have come to view China not simply as a dynamic, ambitious competitor, but as a dangerous rival increasingly alien in its values, and bent on shaping a future Sino-centric global order far different from the one desired by the West.[19]

This change in outlook has colored the West's views of China's global economic and technological expansion. The first set of concerns revolve around the European piece of China's $USD

17. "China Presses Its Internet Censorship Efforts Across the Globe," *New York Times*, March 2, 2018, https://www.nytimes.com/2018/03/02/technology/china-technology-censorship-borders-expansion.html.

18. United Nations Committee on the Elimination of Racial Discrimination, *Consideration of Reports Submitted by States Parties Under Article 9 of the Convention: China*, April 18, 2017.

19. Yan Xuetong, "The Age of Uneasy Peace: Chinese Power in a Divided World," *Foreign Affairs*, Jan.–Feb. 2019; Oriana Skylar Mastro, "The Stealth Superpower: How China Hid its Ambitions," *Foreign Affairs*, Jan.–Feb. 2019.

one-trillion Belt and Road Initiative.[20] China has targeted infrastructure investment into some of the European Union's more economically disadvantaged states, as well as in parts of the Balkans that aspire to future EU accession, through its creation of the "17 + 1" group comprising seventeen Baltic, Balkan, and Eastern European countries and China.[21] A vehicle for Chinese infrastructure and investment financing, the "17 + 1" has also served to fund a massive trade surplus in favor of China among those countries.[22] European officials fear that, over the medium to long term, the "17 + 1" could serve as a geopolitical Trojan horse giving China substantial influence among its much weaker participants, and making it more difficult to achieve consensus within the European Union on China-related issues.

Equally problematic for both Europe and the United States is President Xi's "Made in China—2025," an ambitious plan to give China and its companies global primacy in the technologies of tomorrow: robotics and artificial intelligence, information collection and processing, aerospace, telecommunications, aviation, electric vehicles, pharmaceuticals, and advanced manufacturing

20. https://www.ebrd.com/news/2017/what-chinas-belt-and-road-initiative-means-for-the-western-balkans.html; https://www.nytimes.com/2017/05/13/business/china-railway-one-belt-one-road-1-trillion-plan.html.

21. Jakub Jacobowsky and Marcin Kaczmarsky, *Beijing's Mistaken Offer: The "16+1" and China's Policy Towards the European Union*, OSW Center for European Studies, September 15, 2017, https://www.osw.waw.pl/en/publikacje/osw-commentary/2017-09-15/beijings-mistaken-offer-161-and-chinas-policy-towards-european; Salvatore Balbones, "China's Bid to Buy Eastern Europe on the Cheap: the '16 + 1' Group," *Forbes*, November 27, 2017, https://www.forbes.com/sites/salvatorebabones/2017/11/27/chinas-bid-to-buy-eastern-europe-on-the-cheap-the-161-group/#3ba74c473467.

22. *China's Investment in Influence: The Future of 16 + 1 Cooperation*, European Council on Foreign Relations, December 2016.

technologies.[23] By itself, this strategy would not be an unduly worrisome development, except that it includes a large panoply of systematic policy instruments that could enable China to acquire a commanding lead over key industries and technologies of the future at the expense of everyone else.

One of these is the attempted acquisition by Chinese companies of leading European and US firms—so-called "crown jewels." A case that raised particular alarm was the acquisition in 2016 by Chinese-owned Medea of one of the world's leading robotics firms, the Augsburg-based Kuka. In 2018, Li Shufu, the billionaire chair of Chinese automaker Geely, purchased 9.69 percent of Daimler, raising further concerns. Although many business leaders in Europe and the United States see these activities as part of normal capitalism, they are much more than that. There is no such thing as a Chinese private company, or a Chinese business official, that is independent of the Chinese government or Communist Party. Chinese law makes it an obligation for business entities and individuals to cooperate with intelligence and espionage work whenever requested to do so by the authorities.[24] Recent laws also have increased the degree of Communist Party control at the higher levels of many Chinese companies' boards.[25]

In response, the European Parliament, Council, and Commission have reached a political agreement on an EU framework

23. James McBride, "Is Made in China 2025 a Threat to Global Trade?," *Council on Foreign Relations Backgrounder*, August 2, 2018.

24. Samantha Hoffman and Elsa Kania, "Huawei and the Ambiguity of China's Intelligence and Espionage Laws," *Australian Strategic Policy Institute*, September 13, 2018, https://www.aspistrategist.org.au/huawei-and-the-ambiguity-of-chinas-intelligence-and-counter-espionage-laws/.

25. "China's Communist Party Writes Itself into Company Law," *Financial Times*, August 14, 2017, https://www.ft.com/content/a4b28218-80db-11e7-94e2-c5b903247afd.

for screening foreign direct investment.[26] As Commission President Juncker noted at the time, "we are not naïve free-traders. We need scrutiny over purchases by foreign companies that target Europe's strategic assets."[27] In the United States, CFIUS (Committee on Foreign Investment in the United States), has become quite active in reviewing and blocking proposed Chinese acquisitions in sensitive industries. Yet, both sides acknowledge that there is much more room for closer coordination between the European Union and the United States.[28]

Western officials also have begun to look askance at the commercial activities of Chinese companies that could have a direct bearing on national security, and China's ability to influence a country's political process. For example, the intelligence chiefs of Great Britain and Canada have issued stark warnings against allowing the leading Chinese multinational telecom Huawei to participate in their countries' 5G networks. The United States and Australia already have such a ban in place. Australia has also enacted laws and regulations to limit Chinese acquisitions in sensitive sectors of the economy, including prime agricultural land.[29]

Another area of common focus for further coordination between Europe and the United States is China's vast and growing industrial espionage operations, including widespread cyber-attacks. In 2013, US-based cybersecurity firm Mandiant released

---

26. European Commission—Press Release, *Commission Welcomes Agreement on Foreign Investment Screening Framework,* Brussels, November 20, 2018, http://europa.eu/rapid/press-release_IP-18-6467_en.htm.

27. European Commission—Press Release, *Commission Welcomes Agreement on Foreign Investment Screening Framework.*

28. "Europe and US Agree on Chinese Threat, but Are Too Busy Feuding to Fight It," *New York Times,* December 7, 2018, https://www.nytimes.com/2018/12/07/business/european-union-trump-china-trade.html.

29. See also http://www.imesi.org/2017/06/30/chinese-interferences-australian-politics/.

a report linking the renowned cyber espionage group ATP1 to China's Second Bureau of the People's Liberation Army, and tied it to espionage against 141 victims across multiple industries since 2006.[30] In a late 2018 report submitted to the Senate Intelligence Committee, the US Justice Department claimed that China is involved in 90 percent of all espionage and industrial secrets theft against US entities.[31] Costs to the US economy and companies of all Chinese cyber activities and intellectual property theft range anywhere from US$225 to US$300 billion per year.[32] Other estimates

30. https://www.fireeye.com/blog/threat-research/2013/02/mandiant-exposes-apt1-chinas-cyber-espionage-units.html.

31. "China Involved in 90 Percent of Espionage and Industrial Secrets Theft, Department of Justice Reveals," *Newsweek*, December 12, 2018, https://www.newsweek.com/china-involved-90-percent-economic-espionage-and-industrial-secrets-theft-1255908. See also "A New Old Threat: Countering the Return of Chinese Industrial Cyber Espionage," Council on Foreign Relations Digital and Cyberspace Policy Program, December 6, 2018, https://www.cfr.org/report/threat-chinese-espionage. For a particularly spectacular case of Chinese industrial espionage, see https://www.bloomberg.com/news/features/2018-10-04/the-big-hack-how-china-used-a-tiny-chip-to-infiltrate-america-s-top-companies. China also was likely behind the equally spectacular massive hacking of thousands of sensitive European Union diplomatic cables, "Hacked European Cables Reveal a World of Anxiety about Trump, Russia and Iran," *New York Times*, December 19, 2018.

32. See Peter Harrell, testimony before the Senate Judiciary Committee, "China's Non-Traditional Espionage Against the United States: The Threat and Potential Policy Responses," December 12, 2018; Center for A New American National Security, https://s3.amazonaws.com/files.cnas.org/documents/Harrell-Judiciary-Testimony-December-12-2018-FINAL-min.pdf?mtime=20181211171602. See also Dennis C. Blair and Jon M. Huntsman Jr., "The Report of the Commission on the Theft of American Intellectual Property," National Bureau of Asian Research, May 2013, 3, http://ipcommission.org/report/IP_Commission_Report_052213.pdf; Council of Economic Advisors, "The Cost of Malicious Cyber Activity to the US Economy," The White House, February 2018, 4, https://www.

indicate that industrial espionage and cyber-theft of trade secrets constitute 94 percent of all cyber-attacks, with analysts putting the economic costs to Europe of such cyber espionage at 60 billion euros.[33] In April 2020, in the midst of the COVID-19 pandemic, US officials reported a surge of attacks by Chinese hackers against US healthcare providers, pharmaceutical manufacturers, and the US Department of Health and Human Services. A month later, US officials accused hackers linked to the Chinese government of attempting to steal US research into a coronavirus vaccine.[34]

Clearly, European and American interests overlap substantially across an entire portfolio of issues involving China. In both cases, Chinese companies are aggressively targeting strategic industrial and technological assets for investment stakes or outright acquisition, placing at risk the future economic prosperity and national security of both Europe and the United States. Chinese entities also aggressively target leading European and American companies for intellectual property theft and industrial espionage, often through cyber warfare. Chinese investments in Eastern Europe and the Balkans—and the potential political influence they

---

whitehouse.gov/wp-content/uploads/2018/02/The-Cost-of-Malicious-Cyber-Activity-to-the-US-Economy.pdf . Cited in "Understanding the Chinese Communist Party's Approach to Cyber-Enabled Economic Warfare," Foundation for the Defense of Democracies Report, September 2018.

33. "Europe Raises Flags on China's Espionage," Politico, April 10, 2018, https://www.politico.eu/article/europe-raises-red-flags-on-chinas-cyber-espionage/. "Study on the Scale and Impact of Industrial Espionage and Theft of Trade Secrets through Cyber," report prepared by Price Waterhouse Coopers for the European Commission, Internal Market, Industry, Entrepreneurship and SMEs, April 2018, https://g8fip1kplyr33r3krz5b97d1-wpengine.netdna-ssl.com/wp-content/uploads/2018/10/POLITICO-commission-pwc-scale-and-impact-of-industrial-espionage.pdf

34. https://www.csis.org/programs/technology-policy-program/significant-cyber-incidents.

offer China over the long term—also carry serious risks for the European Union's political coherence, as well as for the NATO alliance, as some of the states most affected are members of both groupings. Closely coordinated strategies among the allies on all these issues will be much more likely to succeed than the efforts so far pursued by the United States and the European Union independent of each other.

Common Economic Interests

Although Donald Trump's threats of a tariff war against Europe obscured the issue, Europe and the United States have far more economic interests in common than whatever else may divide them. As the US Congressional Research Service noted in 2015:

> The United States and the European Union have the largest trade and investment relationship in the world. The relationship generates approximately $5 trillion annually in total commercial sales and provides up to 15 million jobs in the United States and Europe. Merchandise trade totaled approximately $787 billion in 2013. US and European companies are also the biggest investors in each other's markets. Since 2000, 56% of US global investment has gone to Europe. In 2012, more than 70% of total foreign investment in the United States (approximately $1.9 trillion) came from Europe. The total assets of European affiliates in the United States were approximately $8.7 trillion in 2012, and US corporate assets in Europe totaled over $13 trillion. With the United States and the EU together comprising approximately 50% of global gross domestic product (GDP) by value and 40% in terms of purchasing power parity, the transatlantic economic relationship is also the world's most influential in terms of shaping standards and regulations.[35]

35. "The United States and Europe: Current Issues," *Congressional Research Service*, February 3, 2015, https://fas.org/sgp/crs/row/RS22163.pdf.

This massive overlap in common economic interests helps to explain why the European Union and the United States came so close to agreeing on a Transatlantic Trade and Investment Partnership (TTIP) in the last two years of President Obama's administration. Although President Trump's arrival in the White House sank the TTIP along with the Trans-Pacific Partnership, the scale and mutual benefits of EU-US trade and investment links have not changed, and should be the subject of renewed efforts by President Biden's administration.

While the Trump administration spent a great deal of rhetoric on the European Union's alleged unfair practices towards the United States, such atmospherics were unlikely to alter the profoundly positive dynamics linking the two blocs. Indeed, the administration imposed steel and aluminum tariffs on the European Union, threatened a new round of tariffs on EU auto imports, and called for equal access to agricultural products. In response, the European Commission's President Juncker visited Washington in March 2018 and negotiated with President Trump a truce to the brewing trade conflict, even as the US steel and aluminum tariffs remained in place.[36] The new Biden administration has already ended American economic retaliation against the European Union, including tariffs. At the end of the day, the European Union and the United States offer each other something no other country or grouping of states can match: a large affluent market numbering hundreds of millions of people, with an investment and commercial climate subject to the world's most robust legal guarantees and political protections. These realities will outlast the tone or style of any particular administration in Washington.

36. "The European Union: Ongoing Challenges and Future Prospects," *Congressional Research Service*, December 3, 2018, https://fas.org/sgp/crs/row/R44249.pdf.

The American Nuclear Umbrella

A vital interest that holds together the alliance is Europe's need for an effective, credible nuclear deterrent, and the United States' willingness to supply it. Although France and the United Kingdom have nuclear deterrent forces that contribute directly to their own security and indirectly to the Atlantic alliance's stability, they do not provide deterrent protection to any other European state. Only the United States maintains nuclear forces that specifically provide deterrence and defense capabilities for Europe as a whole. In 2017, in the context of then newly elected President Trump's outspoken doubts about the relevance of NATO, European allies wondered whether the United States was any longer a reliable ally willing to extend its nuclear umbrella over Europe.[37] Although senior American officials have subsequently provided plenty of reassurances that the US nuclear umbrella is as sturdy as ever, the debate in Europe has not quieted down completely.

The obstacles to an independent European nuclear deterrent are substantial.[38] Either France or the United Kingdom, or both,

---

37. "Fearing US Withdrawal, Europe Considers Its Own Nuclear Deterrent," *New York Times,* March 6, 2017, https://www.nytimes.com/2017/03/06/world/europe/european-union-nuclear-weapons.html; Jaroslaw Kaczyinski, "Eine Atom Super-Macht Europa würde ich begrüßen," *Frankfurter Allgemeine,* February 6, 2017, https://www.faz.net/aktuell/politik/ausland/polen-kaczynski-macht-werbung-fuer-angela-merkel-14859897.html; Thorsten Benner, "Germany's Necessary Nuclear Debate," Global Public Policy Institute, February 10, 2017, https://www.gppi.net/2017/02/10/germanys-necessary-nuclear-debate.

38. See Oliver Thränert, "No Shortcut to a European Deterrent," *Policy Perspectives* 5, Center for Security Studies, Zurich, 2017, http://www.css.ethz.ch/content/specialinterest/gess/cis/center-for-securities-studies/en/publications/css-policyperspectives/details.html?id=/n/o/s/h/no_shortcut_to_a_european_deterrent; see also Jean-Loup Samaan and David C. Gompert, "French Nuclear Weapons, Euro-Deterrence and NATO," *Contemporary Security Policy* 30 (Dec. 2009): 486–504; Jeffrey Lewis and Bruno Tertrais, "Deterrence at Three: US, UK

would have to make a commitment to extend nuclear deterrence to the Continent. Of the two states, France would be the more likely to do it, though it is far from certain. As is the case now with the US nuclear deterrent, France would have to station nuclear forces in at least several other European countries. The rest of the European allies would have to agree to fund the additional costs associated with broadening and enhancing the French nuclear deterrent. Some analysts believe that France could take up this role well if necessary.[39] Yet, others wonder whether France has sufficient strategic depth to be able to deter credible threats against neighbors in Eastern Europe or the Baltics. Unlike Israel, which seeks to deter threats against its own survival, French survival would not be at stake in a Russian move against Estonia or Romania, and the Russians know this. Well into the distant future, only the United States will be able to provide a sufficiently robust nuclear deterrence to protect North America as well as Europe. The need for such deterrence only will increase as other states around the world, including possibly Iran and some of its Middle Eastern rivals, acquire nuclear weapons over the next decades.

Conclusion

As the world recovers from the COVID-19 pandemic, long-term geopolitical realities will reassert themselves. In spite of initial hopes during its early stages, the pandemic has not made the world a more cooperative place. Nor has the pandemic transformed the serious nature of the challenges that Russia and China pose, in different ways, to Western security and a global order based on

---

and French Nuclear Cooperation," *Survival* 57 (Aug.–Sep. 2015): 29–52; Wilfrid L. Kohl, *French Nuclear Diplomacy* (1971); Brad Roberts, *The Case for US Nuclear Weapons in the 21st Century* (2016).

39. Vipin Narang, *Nuclear Strategy in the Modern Era: Regional Powers and International Conflict* (2014).

liberal, democratic values. The need for the US-European alliance has never been greater. The Biden administration—in spite of alienating European allies through its ill-conceived Afghan withdrawal and its mismanagement of AUKUS—will have plenty of opportunities to renew that alliance. Powerful long-term trends and security needs on both sides of the Atlantic will also play a role. The post-pandemic world will be much safer, not through rhetorical commitments to "global governance" by virtue-signaling Western elites, but through a strengthening of the alliance between the United States and Europe. Such strengthening should be part of a long-term process that also encompasses "the wider West" by forging stronger links with states in Asia and elsewhere that share the alliance's geopolitical interests and fundamental values.

4

The Grace of Law and Natural Law in Times of Crisis

Hon. Rollin A. Van Broekhoven

There is nothing impersonal or theoretical about what I write here. Although I did not discover it at the time, I was in China at the time of the first diagnosis of COVID-19. I am well, but my oldest daughter has suffered with COVID-19 for over five months at the time of writing, and although largely recovered now, still has some residual damage in her bronchial tubes that may take a year to heal completely. I also write as someone who has been in China for well over two years over the past decade teaching in a seminary, lecturing in law schools (including as a visiting professor in a major university in Beijing), working in a law firm, and active in human rights issues.

The common wisdom in the United States, and perhaps worldwide, is that the coronavirus, or COVID-19 is a pandemic that has changed everything. We frequently hear that the "new normal" will not be anything like the "pre-COVID normal." The virus originating in Wuhan, China, spread in a matter of months around the world leading, many countries to experience the largest number of deaths ever. As those who follow the scientific data know, it did not start in a Wuhan wet market as originally reported, but started in a laboratory in Wuhan, notwithstanding disclaimers by the Chinese government, the Chinese Communist Party, and the World Health Organization. The evidence for this is the unique genome structure of the virus itself which could not exist naturally in the animals sold in the wet market. Around the world, each death represented a husband or wife, parent or grandparent, brother or sister, indeed a family. Many countries around the world were essentially shut down to stop the spread of the virus, and the economic well-being of many was adversely affected. Many family members were not permitted to see or say goodbye to their loved ones.

Although I write as an American with many ties in China, and having spent many months in China, the crisis brought forth divisions in our country, although many of these divisions already existed. Our states announced that only essential businesses could remain open or open, and we were told that these decisions were based on science, the new religion of our modern era. So liquor and marijuana stores and bars, for example, were deemed essential while clothing stores and churches were deemed nonessential. Even elective surgery, including serious heart surgery, was considered nonessential and was to be postponed until a later time when opening was permitted. Abortion clinics were deemed essential and could remain open. Churches met, if at all, in viral livestreaming, or occasionally in internet chat rooms or on Zoom. Members have reduced or stopped their giving to the church for various reasons, whether fear of financial need, or the tendency to hoard assets in case they are needed at a later time.

The United States Congress directed the Federal Reserve to create trillion of dollars by fiat, that is, money that was was created electronically to flood banks with liquidity.[1] Such new bailouts have created a whole new sense of government dependency and entitlement. With the loss of livelihood and families sheltering in place, more children are being abused, and there are reports of despair, suicide, drug overdose, and alcoholism.[2]

But it is not just COVID-19. In the United States there is political upheaval, forest fires burning rampantly in the west, hurricanes destroying towns in the east, and tornadoes destroying areas of the midwest. There are descriptions of the horror of massive swarms of grasshoppers blocking the sunlight and eating crops in Ethiopia, Kenya, and Somalia, leaving people to die of starvation in a scene not unlike the biblical plague described in Exodus 10.

Where is God in all of this, and why is he silent? This is the time for us, as believers, to think more deeply about our faith and our role in society that is frightened and hurting, and often without hope.

Although there are many examples throughout human history we could think of, I have been reminded of the 1755 earthquake in Lisbon, Portugal. The earthquake was followed by a tsunami and fires that caused the virtual destruction of all Lisbon, and indeed of the kingdom of Portugal. Eighty-five percent of Lisbon's buildings were destroyed and 30,000 to 40,000 people lost their lives. An additional 10,000 people died in Morocco. Part of the significance of that Lisbon earthquake was that it struck on Sunday morning, November 1—All Saints Day. Theologians, church leaders, and

---

1. Erwin W. Lutzer, *Pandemics, Plagues, and Natural Disasters: What Is God Saying to Us?* (Chicago: Moody, 2020); Scott Pelley, "Coronavirus and the Economy: Best and Worse-Case Scenarios from Minneapolis, Fed. President," CBS News, March 22, 2020.

2. Serena Gordon, "Coronavirus Pandemic May Lead to 75,000 Deaths of Despair from Suicide, Drug and Alcohol Abuse, According to a Study," CBS News, May 8, 2020, htttp://www.cbsnews.com/coronavirus-deaths-suicieds-drugs-alcohol-pandemic-75000.

philosophers speculated whether the devastating earthquake was a manifestation of the anger of God brought about by a city that was filled with sin. Voltaire, who witnessed the earthquake, parodied this line of thinking in a satirical novel, *Candide*. Many found it difficult to reconcile the scope of death and destruction with the idea of a benevolent God. We heard this same concern during the attack on the United States on September 11, 2001.

The Lisbon earthquake was something of a watershed in European theological reflection at the time. *Candide* was Voltaire's way of grappling with the problem of suffering and evil, and proclaiming that the philosophy of "Optimism," the church, and the reigning order of France and Europe were all generally deficient and callous in their response to the human condition. This led to the understanding of science, and specifically geology, as the explanation for such a disaster as the Lisbon earthquake.

While much of what I have written above reflects the scientific laws of nature, human involvement is also at play. Clearly, human action cannot explain all that we have experienced this year, although it does now appear that human action was involved in the Wuhan laboratory, the secrecy on the part of the Chinese government and Communist Party once COVID-19 was discovered, or even in the case of some of the forest fires and the rioting and burning in the US. Since we have no final judgment on the conduct of police officers, I will not address their conduct and whether or not it had anything to do with precipitating the protests and riots. However, as Professor Robert George of Princeton University wrote, "Laws cannot make men moral. Only men can do that, and they do that by freely choosing to do what is the right thing for the right reason."[3] Of course we as Christians know that this is only partially true as I am sure that my friend Robert

---

3. Robert P. George, *Making Men Moral: Civil Liberties and Public Morality* (Oxford: Clarendon, 1993), 1.

George understands. One only needs to read his books to realize that this is the case. Moreover, as he writes, laws can only compel external conformity to some moral principles and laws but cannot compel internal reason and will to make such conformity possible as a moral act.

Similarly, John Finnis, who was basically responsible for the fundamental reshaping of legal philosophy in his book *Natural Rights and Natural Law*,[4] wrote in the introduction to a book of essays he edited, "making, acknowledging, and complying with law involves acts of rational judgment. . . But legal studies are really attractive and worthwhile because law and juristic argumentation is an arena where themes and theses in ethics, political theory, and related philosophical domains all come to bear on—and crystalize out in—legislating and adjudicating to make a difference to human persons."[5]

My interest in this subject arose during my studies in an honors program of jurisprudence over fifty years ago. The major concern I had then and since for more than fifty years has been what I thought was a lack of theological and biblical basis for much of the writing regarding natural law since the Enlightenment. Most of the literature on this topic is traced to Thomas Aquinas, and the social theory is far better developed in Roman Catholic circles, which in my view did not make sufficient room, as I understood it, for the fall or for original sin. Although it has been in the forefront of much of my thinking for all these years, it was not until I started traveling to China to teach jurisprudence in a university law school in Beijing that I was able to focus on natural law, and indeed, on the grace of law as revealed in the Scriptures, especially as I was frequently reminded that China is an atheistic country.

---

4. John Finnis, *Natural Rights and Natural Law* (Oxford: Clarendon, 1980).

5. John Finnis, *Philosophy of Law: Collected Essays, Volume 4* (Oxford: Oxford University Press, 2011), 1.

Wang Zhongfang, writing in the preface of his book, *Forged in Purgatory*:

> From 1967 to 1972, during the unprecedented chaos of the "Cultural Revolution," Lin Biao and the Gang of Four imprisoned me for more than five years. July of 2002 marked 30 years since my release from prison. Memories of the past fade over time and I fear that one day these events will be forgotten. Whenever I open the gate to my memories, however, history appears right in front of my eyes, one scene after another, as if the events of three decades ago just happened yesterday. The troubled times are etched deeply in my memory and eventually I couldn't help but put my thoughts in writing. After much reflection, countless struggles over editing, and many revisions, all geared towards evoking the lessons of the past, this book was created.[6]

Forged in Purgatory is the memoir of Wang Zhongfang. He had held senior positions in China's Ministry of Public Security, Ministry of Justice, the Chinese Communist Party, and the Qinghai Provincial Government. He worked in close proximity with Chairman Mao Zedong until the purges of the Cultural Revolution, when he was imprisoned in Qinghai's maximum-security prison. He was later rehabilitated and dedicated his life to building a legal system and institutions that promoted the rule of law. In his Preface, he wrote: "In the Great Dictionary of the Chinese Language, 'purgatory' is described as a tough environment that makes humans experience great suffering. It is important to me that the ordeals people have undergone amid particular circumstances are recorded for history. Prison, like a steel-making furnace, is truly a form of purgatory."[7]

6. Wang Zhongfang, *Forged in Purgatory* (CreateSpace, 2011), 1.
7. Zhongfang, *Forged in Purgatory*, 1.

What follows in this chapter is an invitation to encourage reflection on where we are today, and especially where China is today. In China, we see the abrogation of the Sino-British Joint Declaration when Britain returned Hong Kong to the Mainland. The Joint Declaration provided for fifty years of continued autonomy from the Mainland with respect to its human rights, government, and independent judiciary. Now, we see the constant rioting against China's abrogation of the Joint Declaration and The Basic Law, which is the Constitution of Hong Kong, as well as the imposition of the new National Security Law that extends China's reach around the world. But we also see the protests, chaos, violence, and destruction in our cities in the United States, and I wonder what happened to our rule of law and our sense that we were once considered a nation under God, with liberty and justice for all.

I write as an American lawyer, a visitor to China, and one who is most interested in China's global position, as well as with Sino-US relationships. I also write as a follower of Jesus Christ. As one who has spent most of his life in the practice of law, it may be asserted that I am ill-equipped to address jurisprudence, which after all is the topic of this chapter. However, my interest goes well beyond Sino-US relationships and China's position in the world. As a result, I write as one looking at China from both outside and within, trying to understand its long history, the history of the ideas that drive China's outlook and position in the world. Yet, I am realistic and realize that very little has been settled for a long time, and that the same uncertainty and potential for change and surprise will continue well into the twenty-first century. Seldom does a day go by that China is not in the news.

The Grace of Law

In this age when it seems that there are no moral standards, at least no universal moral standards, and in which there is confusion about "right" and "wrong," which have lost their absoluteness, the conception of a stable and universal conception of law is absolutely necessary. Indeed, many Christian writers perceive the present moral decay to be due to the neglect of the law of God. Are the Ten Commandments obsolete? Many will answer this in the affirmative for basically two reasons. One of these reasons comes from outside the church due to the cultural shift from negative to positive and the breakdown of a belief in objective moral law. The second comes from within the church and is found in the assumption of many Christians that the teachings of Jesus went far beyond the law of Moses and that the law is no longer binding upon Christians. It is here that one must be careful of thinking in terms of theonomy, and for the United States, Christian reconstructionism. The Puritans began their thinking about this experientially, about the sovereignty of God as the lawgiver. To them, the law must always be the law of God.[8] "The Puritans could never insist too much on the fact that God was the Sovereign of all He had made, with the right to govern all things according to His will. The right to command resided in the majesty of His Person and was expressed in the absoluteness of His will."[9]

The Puritans regarded man has a rational being, not only because he was created in God's image and as such a participant in divine reason which was at the heart of the universe, but also unique in that man alone of all the inhabitants of the earth was aware of divine reason and of his right relationship to the law. Because the moral law was so closely bound by man's rational nature, it was sometimes spoken of as the law of nature, which had a more theological meaning than was found in Stoic philosophy, or even for Thomas Aquinas.

8. Ernest F. Kevan, *The Grace of Law: A Study in Puritan Theology* (Grand Rapids: Soli Dei Gloria, 2018), 47.

9. Kevan, *The Grace of Law*.

My struggle with natural law theory of these past decades has been the naturalistic theory that teaches that all men are able to perceive this law by light of natural reason and do not need specific biblical revelation. Jacques Ellul points out in his *The Theological Foundation of Law* that law by itself, as an autonomous entity, does not exist in the Bible.[10] "The supernaturalistic theory presents a totally different challenge . . . and propounds the view that there is no genuine knowledge of the Law of God except by personal experience of the saving grace of Christ."[11] According to this view, fallen man is totally unable to form any idea of justice and goodness, and therefore, that no such thing as natural law exists. Others suggest that there is a tension due to the ambiguity of "natural law," and so it might be better to speak of "primary" rather than "natural" law.

One of the brighter aspects of Puritan doctrine as the Puritans regarded law, not as burdensome in its original design, but as the essence of man's delight.[12] The Ten Commandments concern human nature and they all make so completely the profit of mankind in this life. If these precepts are observed, men would not need to look to any other human laws. To state it differently,

> The Commandment . . . was given not only for God's sake. . . but for Man's sake, that man might enjoy the good and benefit of his obedience, and find that in keeping the Commands of God there is great reward. . . . A Law emanating from the Divine reason, and given in so direct a manner by God Himself, and for so blessed an end, was held by the Puritans to be nothing less than the very transcript of the glory of God. Man has been made in God's image, and so the moral Law written within him must be part of the very image itself. . . . Their chief reason was the more theological one,

---

10. Jacques Ellul, *The Theological Foundations of Law* (London: SCM, 1960), 45–46.

11. Ellul, *The Theological Foundations of Law*, 57n8.

12. Ellul, *The Theological Foundations of Law*, 60.

that God could not be thought of as requiring anything less than that which accorded with the Divine character.[13]

This brings me to the scope of my long-time reluctance to embrace natural law. The effects of the fall were felt in two ways. First, it dimmed the knowledge and weakened moral ability. Secondly, the Puritans believed that neither of these harmful results was complete and absolute, and that there was sufficient evidence to show that man still had some knowledge of the law and that he still possessed a measure of ability. The awareness of God's law, which was so clear in the heart of man in his innocence, became dimmed through the fall. Nevertheless, although dimmed, there is still a glimmering awareness of the knowledge of the law, by which humans still become aware of sin.

Natural Law Revisited

I have written on the subject of natural law previously with a responsive article by Professor Zhang Shoudong of China University of Political Science and Law, whom I admire greatly.[14] Few people have influenced my thinking on this subject more than have Professors John Finnis, Robert George, Brian Bix, and Ronald Dworkin, all of whom I have written about previously and whom I have admired. My approach here will be different. My interest in jurisprudence is practical because it allows me to read and participate in discussions developing the analytical skills to think critically

---

13. Ellul, *The Theological Foundations of Law*, 61–63.

14. Rollin A. Van Broekhoven, "Morality and Law in a Global Society: A Place for Natural Law Theory," *Frontiers of Law in China* 12, no. 2 (Beijing: Remnin University of China Law School, 2017): 626–72; Zhang Shoudong, "Chinese Natural Law Tradition and Its Modern Application: A Response to Hon. Rollin A. Van Broekhoven," *Frontiers of Law in China* 13, no. 1 (Beijing: Remnin University of China Law School), 86–114.

and creatively about law. As Professor Bix wrote: "jurisprudence is the way lawyers and judges reflect on what they do and what their role is within society."[15] Professor Bix went beyond the idea of a learned profession or trade to the intellectual pursuit of reflective thinking about law, its source and nature, and its role in society. My interest goes deeper to reflective thinking about my faith and how it relates to jurisprudence as described by Professor Bix. Thus, I start with the importance of worldviews in how we think about the world, nature, society, government, and law.

There is probably no greater need for thinking about our worldviews and how they affect our ethics. I draw my philosophy of law largely from the Holy Scriptures, and to a lesser degree from St. Thomas Aquinas. When other writers proudly proclaim themselves as Kantian, Hegelians, Marxist, Benthamites, Platonists, Confucianists, Darwinians, Spinozoists, etc., why should I be ashamed of being a Christian philosopher of law?

The point in my previous article cited above went further than simply a connection between law and morality, which I agree is the case. Rather, failing to explain myself with sufficient clarity, my point is that where we start is where we end up on our analysis of law. As I have thought of our two articles, I have come to the conclusion that there is more than simply a connection between morality and law going on. This has been the focus of my interest and research. What has interested me is how worldviews shape our understanding and application of law, and specifically how the grace of law has affected my thinking of jurisprudence. It is here where I started my reflection on natural law, human rights, and Chinese traditional culture. I come to my position from an assumption that Christianity is divine and greater than all other

15. Brian Bix, *Jurisprudence: Theory and Context,* 2nd ed. (London: Sweet & Maxwell, 1999), ix.

worldviews.[16] John C. H. Wu wrote about the three great religions of China: Buddhism, Taoism, and Confucianism (which is really philosophy or Chinese wisdom literature), and that these came together to serve as his spiritual nurses. Although he profited from all of them, the light he finally saw was the Logos that enlightens every person coming into the world. The West may be Christian and have a Christian history, but Christianity is not Western. It is beyond East and West, beyond the old and the new. As John C. H. Wu wrote: "It is older than the old, newer than the new. It is more native to me than the Confucianism, Taoism, and Buddhism in whose milieu I was born. I am grateful to them, because they served as pedagogues to lead me to Christ. Christ constitutes the unity of my life. It is thanks to this unity that I can rejoice in being yellow and educated white."[17]

John C. H. Wu wrote many years ago that when we speak of law, we ordinarily mean human law, the law that regulates transactions and the rights and obligations, civil and criminal responsibility, and prescribes remedies for wrongdoing.[18] Therefore, why should we bring such things as theology, philosophy, ethics, sociology, and economic theories into the mix? For one thing, law is not simply a craft or business for making a living as too many lawyers and laymen think. The remoter and general aspects of law are those which give universal interest. "It is through them that you not only become a great master of your calling, but connect your subject to the universe and catch an echo of the infinite, a glimpse of its unfathomable process, a hint of the universal law."[19]

16. John C. H. Wu, *Beyond East and West* (New York: Sheed and Ward, 1951), 12.

17. Wu, *Beyond East and West*, 12.

18. John C. H. Wu, *Fountain of Justice: A Study in the Natural Law* (New York: Sheed and Ward, 1955), 4.

19. Wu, *Fountain of Justice*, 5.

Herman Dooyeweerd argued that there are two basic types of worldviews, and that the essential components determined the difference.[20] These are covenantal and non-covenantal. The quest for a worldview has to do with reality, with how we know things, with the purpose of life, with values and attitudes, and with guidance of thought.

Worldviews do a number of things relevant to law. They ground life in a confessed ultimate reality. They relate life to the universal order of existence. They serve as an interpretative/integrative framework for all of life. They are stored and expressed in symbols. They evoke emotional attitudes and moods of deep satisfaction, joy, and inner peace. They induce intellectual assent and deepen conceptual reflection. We come at our worldviews from a lot of different ways. Most of the time, we don't even think about them or the force they have in our lives. But, when they are challenged, no matter what the worldview may be, the challenge can be very frightening and threatening to the very core of our beings. How and why does this happen?

Christians are by no means alone in rejecting modernity's claim to intellectual neutrality. The postmodern mind defines itself over against the modern, and claims a place at the table for a plurality of perspectives, be they gender-based, ethnic, or whatever. But the Christian objection is more premodern than postmodern; it is basically Augustinian in that faith seeks understanding and wisdom of God is both the objective locus of truth and the ultimate sources for all human knowledge.[21]

---

20. Herman Dooyeweerd, *Encyclopedia of the Science of Law,* trans. Robert D. Knudsen (Grand Rapids: Paideia, 2012), 21–85; *Roots of Western Culture: Pagan, Secular, and Christian Options,* trans. John Kraay (Grand Rapids: Paideia, 2012), 7–25.

21. David K. Naugle, *Worldview: The History of a Concept* (Grand Rapids: Eerdmans, 2002), xiii–xiv.

The Christian understanding of creation leads directly to the conclusion that there is a correspondence between the Works of God and the Being of God.[22] As Professor Alister McGrath of the University of Oxford points out, "Creation and redemption are not merely interconnected within the economy of salvation; they can be argued to embody the character of God."[23]

Professor Hadley Arkes wrote that:

> When we contemplate those things that stand, universally as good or bad, justified or unjustified, we are in the domain of morals (or ethics); and as Aristotle understood, the matter of ethics is irreducibly, a *practical* concern: ethics involves an understanding of the standards that ultimately guide our practice or the activities of our daily lives. Those standards, of necessity, are abstract; if they are not, they could not be universal in their application. There is nothing "empirical" about them. . . . The act of legislating [or judicial decisionmaking] would stand out as a massive act of presumption unless it were understood that there are in fact propositions with universal reach, which define what is good or bad, just or unjust, for people in general.[24]

Judgments on law, whether in the academy, the legal profession, or the public in general, seem to imply the existence of moral principles on which moral judgments are founded and justified if they were regarded to be valid and comprehensive. However, they have not taken as their mission or concern the task of actually making clear the nature of the principles on which their judgments rest. Yet in the circles in which such things are considered and discussed, the most widely expressed fallacy is the notion that the

22. Alister E. McGrath, *A Scientific Theology, Vol 1: Nature* (Grand Rapids: Eerdmans, 2001), 193–204.

23. McGrath, *Scientific Theology*, 1:193.

24. Hadley Arkes, *First Things: An Inquiry into the First Principles of Morals and Justice* (Princeton: Princeton University Press, 1986), 3–4.

presence of disagreement on matters of morals must indicate the absence of universal truths. What we are left with is the arbitrary action of executives, legislators, Party members, or judges. At the same time, although there may be disagreements between mathematicians over proofs or conclusions, there is nothing in their disagreements to challenge the foundation of mathematical truths or to call into question the possibility of knowing mathematical truths.

Romans 1–2 is quite clear that the universe is a revelation of the power and deity of God. Thus, from Romans 1:18–20:

> For the wrath of God is revealed from heaven against all ungodliness and unrighteousness of men who suppress the truth in unrighteousness, because that which is known about God is evident within them; for God made it evident to them. But since the creation of the world, His invisible attributes, His eternal power and divine nature, have been clearly seen, being understood through what was made, so that they are without excuse.

But it is more than that, for as we read in Romans 2:14, "the Gentiles who do not have the law do instinctively the things of the law." The use of the word *instinctively* suggests that by natural impulse without external constraints of the Mosaic law, they fulfill the practices of the law that agreed with the law. As Romans 1:24 states: "Wherefore God also gave them up to uncleanness through the lusts of their own hearts, to dishonor their own bodies between themselves; who changed the truth of God into a lie, and worshipped and served the creature more than the Creator." But the text continuing in Romans 1:28–32 states:

> And just as they did not see fit to acknowledge God any longer, God gave them over to a depraved mind, to do those things which are not proper, being filled with all unrighteousness, wickedness, greed, evil; full of envy, murder, strife, deceit, malice; they are gossips, slanderers haters of God, insolent, arrogant, boastful,

inventors of evil, disobedient to parents, without understanding, untrustworthy, unloving, unmerciful; and though they know the ordinance of God, that those who practice such things are worthy of death, they not only do the same, but also give hearty approval to those who practice them.

This is not written only for the benefit of or criticism of the Jews. It was written to all people. It is clear that corruption is not a unique phenomenon in China, or indeed anywhere in the world, whether in the East or in the West. Moreover, it is clear that the corruption described may be in violation of the epistemological nature of one's worldview as well as one's metaphysics and axiology.

Since I am interested in Chinese culture, I cannot omit any consideration of Confucius. I have long thought that notwithstanding the presence, power, and authority of the Chinese Communist Party, there is something in the DNA of the Chinese people that includes Daoism and Confucianism. The study of Confucius and his writings raise interesting questions. As an introduction to Confucius' *Analects* states, philosophers who study Confucius are of two minds.[25] On the one hand, Confucius was interested in morals from a moral character perspective. Confucius certainly had more to say about moral character than about moral acts, but that does not mean that the rightness or wrongness of acts were unimportant to his thinking and philosophy. Indeed, Confucius speaks about the *Dao* (or Way) and about *te* (virtue). The way he

---

25. Confucius, *The Analects,* trans. D. C. Lau (London: Penguin, 1979). Too often we think of Confucianism in competition with Christianity. That is not my purpose or view here. Rather, I think of Confucianism as wisdom literature as we think of Plato or Aristotle, and from which we can gain much as we explore the possibility of integrating this deep and powerful tradition of life into our following of Jesus. Gregg A. Ten Elshof, *Confucius for Christians: What an Ancient Chinese Worldview Can Teach Us About Life in Christ* (Grand Rapids: Eerdmans, 2015).

used Dao seemed to cover the sum total of truths about the universe and man, and not only the individual but also the state is said to either possess or not possess the Way. The Way is a highly emotive term and comes very close to *truth* as found in philosophical and religious writings in the West. The word *te*, or virtue, is an endowment humans get from *Heaven*. As a common law lawyer and judge, I found John C. H. Wu perceptive in this regard:

> Christ does not enter into the courtroom as the Lawgiver whose words are legally binding on the judges. No, His kingdom does not belong to this world. The common-law judges have quoted his words as the judges of ancient China would quote the words of Confucius. But as it is impossible to understand the old Chinese jurisprudence without a knowledge of Confucianism, so it is impossible to grasp the spirit of common law without taking account of the permeating influence of Christianity.
>
> In some cases, the Christian influence is so subtle that you cannot put your finger on any specific precept which the Court is applying and yet you feel a Christian atmosphere diffused throughout the opinion.[26]

Mencius, a disciple and interpreter of Confucianism, was an itinerant sage and thought to be a pupil of Confucius's grandson. While we as Christians would disagree with Mencius with respect to human nature, because of our understanding of the fall and original sin, Mencius, unlike Confucius who did not focus on human nature, asserted the innate goodness of the individual believing that it was society's influence or lack of positive cultivating influence that caused bad moral character.

What needs to be said, however, is that in Romans 13:1–8:

---

26. Ten Elshof, *Confucius for Christians*, 174–75n18.

Every person is to be in subjection to the governing authorities. For there is no authority except from God, and those which exist are established by God. Therefore, whoever resists authority has opposed the ordinance of God; and they who have opposed will receive condemnation upon themselves. For rulers are not a cause of fear for good behavior, but for evil. Do you want to have no fear of authority? Do what is good and you will have praise for the same; for it is a minister of God to you for good. But, if you do what is evil, be afraid for it does not bear the sword for nothing; for it is a minister of God, an avenger who brings wrath on the one who practices evil. Therefore, it is necessary to be in subjection, not only because of wrath, but also for the sake of conscience. For because of this you also pay taxes for *rulers* are servants of God, devoting themselves to this very thing. Render to all what is due them, tax to whom tax is *due*, custom to whom custom; fear to whom fear; honor to whom honor.

The text continues with a list of evil acts that repeat essentially the second table of the Decalogue, the opposite of which reflects moral principles.

This leads to the issue of the source and nature of law, and its role in society. Since I have written on the subject of natural law, this section will be brief and additive to what I have already written.[27] The term *natural law* is ambiguous for a number of reasons, which led to some of my reluctance to commit to this theory of legal philosophy. It can refer to the scientific laws of nature, such as gravity or the regularity of the seasons, and it can refer to a type of moral theory as well as a type of legal theory.

According to natural law legal theory, the authority of legal standards is necessarily derived from considerations having to do with the morality of those standards.

---

27. Ten Elshof, *Confucius for Christians*, 174–75n14.

It is a longstanding commonplace in Christian thought that Protestantism distinguishes its moral theology from that of Roman Catholicism by its rejection of natural law. The idea of natural law has long formed the spinal column of Catholic social teaching. Modern Protestantism, by contrast, has no comparable coherent framework for grounding its social thought. As long ago as 1891, on the occasion of one of the great documents of Catholic social teaching, *Rerum Novarum*, the Dutch Reformed theologian conceded the Protestant disadvantage: "It must be admitted to our shame that the Roman Catholics are far ahead of us in their study of the social question. . . . The Encyclical of Leo XIII gives the principles which are common to all Christians, and which we share with our Roman Catholic compatriots. The idea of natural law embodied in the *Rerum Novarum* assumes that there is a universal law to which all people of all races, classes, cultures, and religion have access to by their natural reason. Natural law thus serves as a bridge category on ethical and social questions between the church and the world, between those with *a priori* commitment to sacred Scripture and the Christian creed and those outside the community of faith.[28]

It is important to distinguish between two kinds of theories that go by the name of natural law. The first is where morality is characterized by certain themes, such as moral propositions from sacred texts—for Christians, the Bible—that have objective standards and that can be objectively true or false. The second thesis constituting the core of natural law moral theory is one that claims that standards of morality are sometimes derived from the nature of the world and the nature of human beings. Thus, St. Thomas Aquinas argued that at creation, God produced the soul of man and woman and that a rational soul could not be produced except by God at creation.[29] Since human beings are by nature rational,

28. Carl E. Braaten, "Protestants and Natural Law," *First Things* (January 1992).

29. Thomas Aquinas, *Summa Theologica* I.90.1, 3, trans. Fathers of the English Dominican Province (Westminster, MD: Christian Classics, 1981).

it would be morally appropriate for them to behave in a manner consistent with their rational nature.

Another kind of natural law theory having to do with the relationship between morality and law, suggests that there is no clean division between morality and law. As ambiguous as the term *natural law* may be and as many versions of natural law theory as there are, all of them subscribe to a thesis that there are at least some that depend for their "authority" not on pre-existing human convention but on the logical relationship in which they stand to moral standards. Yet, as we see, some can hold to a natural law theory of morality but deny a natural law theory of law, such as espoused by John Austin who clearly was a positivist. Indeed, Austin inherited his utilitarianism from J. S. Mill and Jeremy Bentham.

But Aquinas and many who follow him (such as Martin Luther King Jr., in his *Letter From a Birmingham Jail*) argued that human law promulgated by governments is valid only if it conforms to the content of natural law. Natural law according to Aquinas is comprised of the precepts of eternal law that govern the behavior of beings possessing reason and free will. The issue here is related to the fall and original sin and the extent to which the fall affected reason and free will.

Blackstone argued that the idea of a norm that does not conform to the natural law cannot be legally valid, since the law of nature being dictated by God himself is superior in obligation to any law made by man, at all times and in all places around the globe.[30]

Classical naturalism is consistent with allowing a substantial role for humans in the promulgation of law. While naturalists seem committed to the claim that the law necessarily incorporates all moral principles, this claim does not imply that the law is exhaust-

---

30. Sir William Blackstone, *Commentaries on the Law of England, Ehrlich's Blackstone* (San Carlos, CA: Nourse, 1959), 7–8.

ed by the set of moral principles. There will still be coordination problems, and of course we have the distinction between *malum in se* and *malum prohibitum* in criminal law. Legal norms are promulgated by human beings and are valid only if they are consistent with morality.

In chapter 2, Professor Finnis sets out the theory of natural law and the objections to it.[31] As I understand him, there are a set of practical principles which indicate the basic forms of human flourishing as goods to be pursued and realized; he is speaking both of the *summum bonum* and the common good that is so prevalent in Christian thinking. At the beginning of Christianity there were a set of moral principles, but not moral philosophy as we would think of it today. This came through St. Augustine of Hippo (354–450), who developed the idea of a rational soul, somewhat consistent with Plato's philosophy. Secondly, according to Finnis, there is a set of basic methodological requirements of practical reasonableness that include human flourishing. The issue I had with the theory was both the definition of *summum bonum* and the effect of the fall or original sin described in Genesis 3 on the power to reason rightly.[32] Further, Finnis asserts more particularly that the principles of natural law explain the obligatory force of positive laws, even when those laws cannot be deduced from those principles.[33]

Finnis, in describing Thomas Aquinas' tackling the question of the extent of human recognition of natural law, opined that Aquinas was working with a threefold categorization of principles or precepts of natural law. First, there are the most general principles that state basic forms of human good, and are recognized by anyone who reaches the age of reason and had enough experience

---

31. Blackstone, *Commentaries on the Law of England*, 7–8n4.
32. Blackstone, *Commentaries on the Law of England*, 23–24.
33. Blackstone, *Commentaries on the Law of England*, 23–24n8.

to know to what they refer. They cannot be eliminated from the heart. Second, even the most elementary and easily recognizable moral implications of those first principles are capable of being obscured or distorted for some people, whether by prejudice, convention, oversight, or desire for immediate gratification. Third, there are many moral questions that can be answered by someone who is wise, and who considers them searchingly.[34]

In response to the question as to whether natural lawyers have shown that they can derive ethical norms from facts, Finnis quickly replies that they have not, nor do they need to, nor did the early proponents of natural law theory attempt to find such derivation. However, he continues:

> Thus it is simply not true that "any form of natural-law theory of morals entails the belief that propositions about man's duties and obligations can be inferred from propositions about his nature." Nor is it true that for Aquinas "good and evil are concepts analyzed and fixed in metaphysics before they are applied in morals." On the contrary, Aquinas asserts as plainly as possible that the first principles of natural law, which specify the basic forms of good and evil and which can be adequately grasped by anyone of the age of reason (and not just metaphysicians), are *per se nota* (self-evident) and indemonstrable. They are not inferred from speculative principles. They are not inferred from facts. They are not inferred from metaphysical propositions, or about the nature of good and evil, or about the function of a human being, nor are they inferred from a teleological conception of nature, or any other conception of natures.[35]

While I am not prepared to debate this point that Finnis makes, as I wrote at the beginning, where our theory of law and our theory of justice take us, it must have a beginning in our

---

34. Blackstone, *Commentaries on the Law of England*, 30.
35. Blackstone, *Commentaries on the Law of England*, 33.

worldviews. While philosophical understanding of metaphysics, epistemology, and axiology help, they do not require philosophical speculation; simply worldview thinking which may be intuitive. I am not a Thomistic scholar and have no claim to the expertise, either in Aristotle's thinking or the writings of St. Thomas Aquinas, reflected in the writings of Professor Finnis. Finnis does identify one of the primary objections to Aquinas's theory of natural law, specifically that "Aquinas fails to explain just how specific moral rules which we need to guide our conduct can be shown to be connected with self-evident principles."[36] He has three answers to this objection. First, the very phrase *natural law* can lead one to assume that there are norms referred to in any theory of natural law, which are based upon some judgments about nature (human or otherwise). Second, this assumption is in fact substantially correct in relation to Stoic theory of natural law. But I would add that according to my understanding, Aquinas brought Stoic philosophy of natural law from Athens together with the Christian teaching out of Jerusalem. Third, Aquinas himself was a writer, not on ethics alone, but on the whole of theology. As Finnis wrote: "He [Aquinas] was keen to show the relationship between his ethics of natural law and his general theory of metaphysics and the world-order."[37]

As I read Germain Grisez, and those who developed and defended his thinking over the past fifty years, such as John Finnis, Joseph Boyle, William May, and Patrick Lee, among others, there are critics who suggest that Grisez's view of the relationship between morality and nature disqualifies his theory of natural law.[38] According to Professor George, Russell Hittinger and others

---

36. Blackstone, *Commentaries on the Law of England*, 34.

37. Blackstone, *Commentaries on the Law of England*, 35.

38. Robert P. George, *Natural Law and Human Nature, Natural Law Theory: Contemporary Essays* (Oxford: Clarendon, 1992), 31.

understand Germain Gresez's theory as failing to interrelate systematically practical reason with a philosophy of nature. Professor George continues asserting that a problem with the criticism of Lloyd Weinreb is that he argues that Grisez and his collaborators, including Finnis, rely on implausible claims that certain propositions in normative ethics and political theory are self-evidently true.[39] Professor George mentions another critic of Grisez and his collaborators as erecting a wall of separation between practical reason and theoretical reason, between ethics and metaphysics, between nature and morals, between "is" and "ought," arguing that Grisez and Finnis, among others, "maintain the absolute independence of ethics over against metaphysics, or of morals with respect to knowledge of nature." As a result, principles of morals and of ethics are not thought of as being principles of being or of nature at all.[40] However, as I read Professor George's thinking, I understand him to argue that the theory's denial that practical knowledge (including knowledge of moral norms) can be inferred from methodologically antecedent knowledge of human nature does not entail the proposition that moral norms are unrooted in human nature.[41]

As I read the magisterial reformers of the Protestant Reformation, this perspective of natural law appeared to be widely accepted in their own time. Moreover, it answers the question I often pose as to whether the law was pre-political, or whether it is granted by government with all of its rights and obligations defined by government. We read in John 1:17 that "For the Law was given through Moses; grace and truth were realized through

---

39. George, *Natural Law and Human Nature*, 31–32, citing Lloyd Weinreb, *Natural Law and Justice* (Cambridge, MA: Harvard University Press, 1987), 112–13.

40. George, *Natural Law and Human Nature*, 32.

41. George, *Natural Law and Human Nature*, 30–41.

Jesus Christ." The question then arises: If natural law is merely a body of precepts that are self-evident principles of justice written on the hearts of human beings, what then is its contribution to jurisprudence? "The refinement of natural law is called culture."[42]

Confucius' teaching corresponds to the thinking of St. Thomas Aquinas, who saw the eternal law, the natural law, and human law as forming a continuous series. What was ordained by heaven was the plan of divine providence, which included natural law. The refinement of the natural law is the task of culture, which includes human law and manners. Aquinas and Confucius both reached practically the same result about natural law based on natural reason as a bridge between eternal law and human law without the aid of revelation.

The essence of law is justice, which all existing laws should endeavor to embody as perfectly as possible. Aristotle said that justice is the most excellent of virtues. In Christian teaching, love is more noble than justice, but among the moral virtues, love is but a higher form of justice. Further, Wu addresses the issue of justice and truth as follows:

> Truth enters into the philosophy of law on two different planes. First, on the metaphysical plane, we must visualize the human law as a rivulet flowing from the natural law, which in turn, flows from the eternal law. The fountainhead of all law is God. If we do not realize this, then we are not true realists, but blind gropers in the realm of passing shadows. . . .
>
> Secondly, on the empirical plane, we must see law in its relation to the other sciences and actualities of life.
>
> The first requisite of a just judgment is that it must be based upon the facts. In fact, the popular notion of justice is inseparably bound up with truth. Our imagination is excited

---

42. George, *Natural Law and Human Nature*, 219.

and our hearts cheered up when, whenever we observed that truth is found out in a puzzling case.[43]

No paper on natural law would be complete without some discussion of Professor Ronald Dworkin's contribution to jurisprudence. As a friend of many years and a reader of all he wrote, I probably am not the one to comment on his contributions to natural law, assuming for a moment that he does espouse natural law theory. Perhaps it is simply because he did not fit into my understanding of the topic, which may say more about me and my understanding of natural law than about him, and because we had significantly different political philosophies on a large number of issues. Nevertheless, he was always engaging, and tested his thinking in public forums before revising them for final publication. I first read Dworkin's writings in 1975 as a lawyer with an interest in jurisprudence and then as a federal trial judge.[44] Since then, I have read and studied all of his books, taken seminars under him at the University of Oxford, and had multiple discussions with him.

One way to start is to state his thesis, as he expressed it in 1977 in his book, *Taking Rights Seriously*.[45] It is generally clear from his writings that he disagrees with legal positivists who, according to Dworkin, "generally assumed that the law of a political community comprised a set of rules whose primary function was to specify the forms of social behavior which were liable to coercive sanctions inflicted by the government authority."[46] According

43. George, *Natural Law and Human Nature*, 240–41n18.

44. Ronald Dworkin, "The Model of Rules," *University of Chicago Law Review* 35 (1967); and "Hard Cases," *Harvard Law Review* 88 (1975).

45. Ronald Dworkin, *Taking Rights Seriously* (Cambridge, MA: Harvard University Press, 1977).

46. Charles Covell, *The Defense of Natural Law: A Study of the Ideas of Law and Justice in the Writings of Lon L. Fuller, Michael Oakeshot, F. A. Hayek, Ronald Dworkin, and John Finnis* (London: MacMillan, 1992), 146–95.

to Covell interpreting Dworkin, the positivist assumed that rules of law were always identifiable by certain criteria of legal validity, which stood as tests or standards concerned not with the substantive content of such rules, but with the manner in which they were proscribed or adopted by judicial and political institutions in the given community.[47]

As a judge, I was particularly interested in Dworkin's *Law's Empire*, in which he treated judges almost as philosopher-rulers adjudicating hard cases according to some existing principles, rather than simply legal rules.[48] He sets out his thesis of the importance of law and why it matters in the first pages:

> It matters how judges decide cases. It matters most to the people unlucky or litigious or wicked or saintly enough to find themselves in court. . . . Criminal cases are the most frightening of all, and they are the most fascinating to the public. But civil suits, in which one person asks compensation or protection from another for some past or threatened harm, are sometimes more consequential than all but the most momentous criminal trials. The difference between dignity and ruin may turn on a single argument that might have not struck another judge so forcefully, or even the same judge on another day. . . .
>
> Lawsuits matter in another way that cannot be measured in money or even liberty. There is an inevitable moral dimension to an action at law, and so as standing risk of a distinct form of public injustice. A judge must decide not just who shall have what, but who has behaved well, who has met the responsibilities of citizenship, and who by design or greed or insensitivity has ignored his own responsibilities to others or exaggerated theirs to him. If this judgment is unfair, then the

47. Covell, *The Defense of Natural Law*, 146.

48. Ronald Dworkin, *Law's Empire* (Cambridge, MA: Harvard University Press, 1986).

community has inflicted a moral injury on one of its members because it has stamped in some dimension an outlaw. The injury is gravest when an innocent person is convicted of a crime, but it is substantial enough when a plaintiff with a sound claim is turned away from court or a defendant leaves with an undeserved stigma.[49]

Thus, for Dworkin, the theory of adjudication implicit in the positivist model of law could not be reconciled with the legitimate role played by legal principles in the judicial decisions in "hard cases." According to Professor George, Dworkin's "rights theory" related to individual rights that constrained the government's pursuit of collective interests.[50] It is clear that according to this thinking, individual rights will often be in conflict with community interests and the common good. In my reading of Dworkin's writings and in countless discussions, Dworkin endorses what he understands as liberal positions which are often in conflict with traditional, historical morality as understood generally, except in cases of extraordinary emergency. As a result, individual rights, as defined by Dworkin, almost always trump collective interests and what many have considered the common good.

The issues I have long had with Dworkin's rights theories and which we have discussed are clearly stated by Professor George in *Making Men Moral.* From where do these individual rights come or how are they derived? My worldview thinking has clearly placed the source and nature of these rights and, indeed, obligations in God's providence, in his creation of man and woman in his image, and the understanding of these rights and obligations for advancing the common good from natural revelation, special revelation,

49. Dworkin, *Law's Empire*, 1–2.

50. Robert P. George, *Making Men Moral: Civil Liberties and Public Morality* (Oxford: Clarendon, 1993), 85.

and from Jesus Christ. Of course, not all will come to this conclusion, and because of the fall and original sin, we are incapable of objective reason. As Professor George wrote:

> Whether the specific political rights favored by Dworkin and other liberals can plausibly be derived from this abstract right is questionable. I challenge below Dworkin's proposed derivation of one such right, namely the right of "privacy" or "moral independence" [the basic cause of original sin or the Fall and ejection from the Garden of Eden]. For now, I simply wish to observe that the abstract right to equality appears foundational to Dworkin's theory of political morality—he makes no effort to derive it from more fundamental principles. But this lack of a derivation is problematic in that the proposition appears to be neither a self-evident practical principle nor a necessary truth of any kind.[51]

Professor Dworkin raised a challenge in his *Justice for Hedgehogs*.[52] He poses the question of whether we can talk about values, such as how to treat other people, unless we start with bigger philosophical issues. He then asks where values come from. God? But what if there is no God? Can values just be out there, part of what there really, finally is? He points out that even friends disagree on what is right or wrong.[53] He argues that ancient moral philosophers, such as Plato and Aristotle, saw the human situation as one in which we have lives to live and want to live those lives well; where ethics commanded us to seek happiness in the fulfillment of life conceived as a whole, and morality had commands that are captured in a set of virtues that included justice. But he continues:

---

51. George, *Making Men Moral*, 85–86.

52. Ronald Dworkin, *Justice for Hedgehogs* (Cambridge, MA: Harvard University Press, 2011).

53. Dworkin, *Justice for Hedgehogs*, 23.

The god-intoxicated philosophers of the early Christian period and of the Middle Ages had the same goal, but they had been given—or so they thought—an obvious formula for achieving it. Living well means living in God's grace, which in turn means following the moral law God had laid down as the law of nature. The formula was the happy consequence of fusing two conceptually distinct issues how people have come to hold their ethical and moral beliefs, and why those ethical and moral beliefs are correct. God's power explains the genesis of the conviction; we believe what we do because God has revealed to us directly or through the powers of reason he created in us. . . . The formula did not make for entirely smooth sailing. The Christian philosophers were troubled above all by what they called the problem of evil. If God is all-powerful and the very measure of goodness, why is there so much suffering and injustice in the world?[54]

One of the problems I have had with Dworkin's thinking over the years has been that I have never been really convinced that he was an adherent of natural law. As stated by Professor George and others, his beliefs appear to result from a form of utilitarianism, which he calls "neutral or collective utilitarianism" as a working conception of his collective interests in American politics. While I do not doubt that some legislators or judges appeal to utilitarianism and consequentialism, I agree with Professor George and others, including Professor Grisez and Finnis, that these attempts are futile.[55]

The new national security law, which bars what is called sedition, subversion, terrorism, and colluding with foreign forces, allows China to pursue and prosecute people seen as violating the

54. Dworkin, *Justice for Hedgehogs*, 16.

55. See Dworkin, *Justice for Hedgehogs*, 88n3; see also Germain Grisez, "Against Consequentialism," *American Journal of Jurisprudence* 23 (1978); and John Finnis, *Fundamentals of Ethics* (Oxford: Oxford University Press, 1983), 86–93.

law, even outside of Hong Kong. A naturalized US citizen from Hong Kong, Samuel Chu, who has lived in the US for thirty years and been an American citizen for twenty-five years, was reported as being on the list of fugitives sought under the law after he lobbied the US Congress to punish China for eroding Hong Kong's autonomy.

Although the news media is filled with reports of protests and violence in major US cities and it is clear that the United States has much to do to clean up its own problems, the question arises in my mind as to the justification for China to extend its jurisdiction both with respect to laws and enforcement of those laws beyond its own territories. The same applies to both its activity in the South China Sea with respect to its construction of islands, primarily for military bases, in international waters. What seems particularly inconsistent with the long history of China is its Belt and Road Initiative, or BRI. Since its inception in 2013, 136 countries and 39 international organizations have signed on to BRI, receiving US$90 billion in Chinese foreign direct investment and exchanged US$6 trillion in trade with China. While China has failed to present a clear narrative for the initiative, social movements and affected communities and non-governmental organizations around the world have criticized BRI for its harmful environment affects, social and economic impacts, and resisted their implementation. As an observer of BRI since its inception, I have often wondered whether the recipient countries will ever be able to pay China for the loans and investments, and the extent of Chinese economic and political influence in these countries. But further discussion of that is beyond the scope of this chapter.

Conclusion

I conclude where I started. I am an American lawyer, and a frequent visitor to China who is interested in China's global position as well as with Sino-American relationships. But it is more than that. I write as one looking from the outside into China trying to understand its long history, the history of the ideas that drive China's outlook and position in the world. I am simply an observer and recognize that the subjects touched in this paper affect all countries, including the United States of America, although the topic of the conference at which an earlier version of this chapter was presented addressed natural law theory, human rights, and the traditional Chinese cultural context.

However, as an observer, I am able to draw a number of conclusions from what I have observed and reasoned. While it seems clear that the coronavirus started in Wuhan, and specifically in the Wuhan laboratory, and that the Chinese government and the Chinese Communist Party hid the details of the virus from the rest of world thereby allowing it to spread to a pandemic, it is unclear whether the creation of the virus was an intentional wrong and a violation of the chemical/biological international agreements and Geneva Convention or simply the result of negligence.

Moreover, it seems quite clear under international law that China's activities in Xinjiang Province, Hong Kong, Tibet, and the South China Sea violate international norms regarding human rights and religious freedom. While much might be said about the Belt and Road Initiative, this is not the place to say it, although it does seem clear that China is using its economic power to subject countries to Chinese authority and desire. What is clear, however, is that China has not been consistent in experiencing the grace of law and of basing its legal system and alleged rule of law on natural law theory.

However, we in Western societies are not free from fault. While there is still question about the source of some of the fires on the US West Coast, it does seem clear at the present that a number of them are caused by humans, either through carelessness or arson, and that most of the forest fires in the West are due to poor forest management. What is quite clear is that while some protest activity may be constitutionally protected speech, the violence, rioting, and destruction of businesses and private property are not. Regardless of the form of government and of law, there are certain principles that must be kept in mind. There is no doubt that Christianity, and perhaps natural law, are imperiled by two great and serious dangers.[56] Two worldviews are wrestling with each other in mortal combat. Modernism is bound to build a world of its own from the data of natural man. On the other hand, those who bend their knee in worship to Jesus Christ, as the Son of the living God, are bent to save the Christian heritage. Today, postmodernity plays a role in the sense that there is no truth and that all that counts is the experiences which we have from day to day. This has been the struggle in Europe, and now in America. Regardless of the particular form of government, in Calvin's view all subjects of the state are responsible for their own obedience.[57]

Do believers have the biblical or theological justification to rebel against bad rulers because of their poor or evil leadership? Calvin recognized the nature of man to rebel against evil rulers. However, for Calvin, submission to governing authorities was non-negotiable. He insisted that that our respect for the Word of God would require no less and would lead us to further be subject to their authority, as well as that of lower magistrates, who might honestly and faithfully perform their duties toward us. Of course, many in the time of Calvin, just as today, do not do so. Calvin had a response to that, arguing that we still owe the respect to office. For Calvin, a failure for a believer to submit to bad governments

56. Abraham Kuyper, *Lectures on Calvinism* (Grand Rapids: Eerdmans, 1931), 11.

57. G. Joseph Gatis, "The Political Theory of John Calvin," *Bibliotheca Sacra* 1953 (Oct.–Dec. 1996), 449, 459–60.

simply because they were bad could justify the destruction of other important societal structures.[58]

Beyond Calvin's argument for submission to tyrants was his argument that the believer's submission to bad rulers and tyrants was practical because the right of government is ordained by God for the well-being of mankind and for the preservation of legitimate order and part of God's sovereign plan.[59] Again we see how the sovereignty of God was central to Calvin's thought. As a result, although tyrants may assume absolute authority, they still derive their authority and powers from God, and are ultimately accountable to him. It seems clear from recent history in China that the principles of natural law have not been adequately followed and that human rights are not respected notwithstanding the language in the Constitution of the People's Republic of China. But my argument goes beyond China and encompasses the West. We in the West are not free from guilt and the effects and nature of the fall. Whether in China or in the rest of the world, salvation is by grace alone, by faith alone, and that righteousness we may have is imputed by God to us. However, what we see in this pandemic, and in the disasters produced in nature, whether tornados and hurricane, or locusts, is that many are the result of human rejection of the grace of law and natural law.

Yet, we do not dare end on a totally negative note. God is at work in the world as he always has been. Despite persecution, both "family" churches and "registered" churches are meeting regularly. I receive by social media and email Bible studies, scheduled Bible reading, and prayer requests everyday from China. There are churches that are praying daily for my daughter who has suffered with COVID-19 for the last five months. I am able to teach, mentor, and disciple judges, law professors, lawyers, and law students,

---

58. Gatis, "Political Theory of John Calvin," 449.
59. Gatis, "Political Theory of John Calvin," 449.

whether online through video chat, or in person in Beijing, as well as elsewhere in China. God has opened up journals in which my writings can be published in China.

The story is told of a Chinese student, Joshua [not his real name], who while in the United States studying at a major university, came to Christ and served as a volunteer working with Chinese students until he returned to China. When he told his father that he considered staying in the United States, his father was deeply grieved by the long distance. This caused Joshua to realize a profound spiritual truth—if an earthly father felt this much grief in separation from his child, how great was the pain of separation between our heavenly Father and those who might have known him. As a result of this realization, Joshua felt a strong calling to return to China so that he could help people come to know Jesus. Because of his flexible work schedule, Joshua was able to volunteer serving Chinese students returning from abroad. Among returning Chinese students and scholars, including those with whom I work, there are many challenges. The challenges are even more significant and complex for the new believers who return to their home country. I have seen how easy it is in a materialistic world for these returning scholars to drift away.

The point is that God is at work in the midst of a global pandemic. When COVID-19 emerged, Christians in China were quick to respond. Churches took the initiative to send masks and food supplies to Wuhan. They also established "prayer altars," with daily meetings praying for people, including my daughter, around the world, not just in China. Throughout all of this we see the grace of law, and even natural law at work in China, as we seek it at work around the world. As C. S. Lewis wrote, "Pain is God's megaphone to rouse a deaf world."[60]

---

60. C. S. Lewis, *The Problem of Pain: How Human Suffering Raises Almost Intolerable Intellectual Problems* (New York: Macmillan, 1962), 93.

5

Pandemic, International Trade, and US-China Relations

Michael Tai

Development of International Trade

Phoenicians, Egyptians, Greeks and Syrians engaged in trade around the Mediterranean as early as the third millennium BC. Roman coins minted in the first century AD found in China testify to trade between the Roman Empire and the Han Empire of China. The ancient Silk Road was not a single route, but a network of roads across central Asia to Europe which enabled economic, cultural, political and religious interaction across Eurasia from the second century BC to the eighteenth century. Travel along the route was risky until the Mongols established their rule (Pax Mongolia) across the continent. In the early fifteenth century, the Portuguese found sea routes to the East and led to the rise of European colonialism. The most recent phase of international trade which began in the postwar era saw the establishment of rules of trade. The General Agreement on Trade and Tariffs (GATT) boosted post-war economic recovery by reducing tariffs, quotas and subsidies. Despite deficiencies due to the asymmetry in market power between developed and developing countries, GATT and its successor, the World Trade Organization (WTO), spurred the expansion of international trade and the process of globalization.

Globalization led to greater interdependence of the world's economies, but there were winners and losers depending on how successfully individual states managed their trade and investment activities. Latin America and Africa became worse off whereas some East Asian economies have done better. The World Bank and the International Monetary Fund (IMF) played key roles in shaping international trade and investments. The World Bank was set up as a development bank to provide loans and grants for roads, railways, power plants, hospitals and schools in order to raise employment, incomes and living standards. The IMF's role, on the other hand, was to monitor the balance of payments as well as the monetary and exchange rate policies of member states with a view to maintain financial stability. But both institutions have been criticized for doing more harm than good through structural adjustment programs which hurt the poor disproportionately.[1] By opening their doors to foreign direct investments (FDI) and restricting short-term capital flows, East Asian states such as Malaysia, Singapore, Taiwan, Japan and South Korea achieved better results. China is one of the biggest beneficiaries of globalization; since opening up to foreign trade and investments in 1979, its GDP has grown by an average of 9.5% per annum—what the World Bank describes as "the fastest sustained expansion by a

1. William Easterly, "IMF and World Bank Structural Adjustment Programs and Poverty," in *Managing Currency Crises in Emerging Markets* (University of Chicago Press, 2003), 361–92.

major economy in history."[2] It has been the world's largest exporter of goods since 2009 and the largest trading nation since 2013. China's main trading partners are its closest neighbors, Japan and South Korea, but it also conducts a significant amount of trade with the US and Europe. China, EU and the US together account for almost half of world trade in goods (46% of global exports and 45% of global imports) with their respective shares of world exports being: China 17%, EU 16%, and the US 14%.[3] China's rapid economic growth stems from large-scale capital investment and rapid productivity growth. As with other East Asian economies, the Chinese state uses "industrial policy" to channel resources into key sectors. Chinese economic management prefers pragmatism over ideology, an attitude encapsulated by Deng Xiaoping's dictum that "it doesn't matter whether a cat is black or white, as long as it catches mice." When the United States and China normalized relations in 1970s, policymakers in Washington debated the means of converting China and bringing it into the Western fold. Would the Chinese forsake communism and embrace capitalism? No one could have foreseen at the time the extent to which the country would integrate into the US-led economic order. But instead of celebrating the outcome, Washington now sees China as a threat.

US-China Relations

US-China relations has gone through twists and turns. In August 1784, the *Empress of China* docked in Guangzhou, marking America's entrance into the lucrative China trade in tea, porcelain, and

2. "China's Economic Rise: History, Trends, Challenges, and Implications for the United States," accessed August 16, 2020, https://www.everycrsreport.com/reports/RL33534.html.

3. "The EU, USA, and China Account for Almost Half of World Trade in Goods," accessed August 15, 2020, https://ec.europa.eu/eurostat/web/products-eurostat-news/-/DDN-20170824–1?inheritRedirect=true.

silk. On board was Samuel Shaw, an unofficial consul appointed by the US Congress, but he failed to make contact with Chinese officials or gain diplomatic recognition for the United States. Official diplomatic relations did not begin until sixty years later with the 1884 Treaty of Wangxia which granted extraterritoriality for US citizens (giving US citizens immunity from Chinese law) and most-favored-nation status. Following the outbreak of the California Gold Rush in 1848, Chinese laborers arrived to work in mines, on railroads, and in other menial work. Within the first twenty years, over 100,000 came, and some 20,000 took part in the construction of the Transcontinental Railroad. It was back-breaking labor in frigid winters and blazing summers, and hundreds died from explosions, landslides, accidents and disease. But the Chinese came to be seen by white Americans as an economic threat, and after more than a decade of anti-Chinese lobbying, Congress passed the Chinese Exclusion Act in 1882, barring Chinese immigration into the United States.[4] There were other forms of exclusion. On September 2, 1885, a white mob set upon Chinese miners in Rock Springs, Wyoming, killing twenty-eight and destroying their property. This sparked a wave of assaults in other parts of America over the next several years. To discourage Asians from settling permanently, alien land laws were passed which limited the ability of Asians to own land and property.

The geopolitical landscape in East Asia changed dramatically at the turn of the twentieth century. While China struggled to fend off Western encroachment, Japan modernized through a series of bold reforms and stunned the world by defeating China (1895) and Russia (1904–1905). The victories changed the balance of power in the Far East, and to check Japanese expansion into

---

4. In Canada, the Chinese Immigration Act of 1885 levied a $50 head tax on Chinese immigrants entering Canada. $50 or the equivalent of over $1,000 today was a hefty amount for impoverished Chinese laborers in the nineteenth century.

China and Southeast Asia, Washington imposed an oil embargo on Japan in 1941. Japan responded by attacking Pearl Harbor and invading the Philippines, a US colony, drawing America into the war as an ally of China. Following the communist victory in the Chinese Civil War in 1949, America refused to recognize the new government in Beijing and imposed a trade embargo. Relations further deteriorated during the Korean War. Sino-US relations took another turn twenty years later when Washington sought Beijing's help to withdraw from Vietnam.[5] This led to rapprochement and the lifting of the trade embargo. In the 1972 Shanghai Communiqué, both sides agreed to "facilitate the progressive development of trade between the two countries."[6] In 1978, the Chinese Communist Party renounced class struggle and took up economic development as its central focus.[7] China and the US once again became allies, this time against the Soviet Union, but the instrumental partnership lasted only until the fall of the Soviet Union in 1991. America emerged as the sole superpower, and China's usefulness diminished. By this time, China had implemented market reforms and opened up to world trade, although it was still poor and backward with a GDP of $360 billion or one-sixteenth of America's $6 trillion economy. After a lengthy process of negotiations and further required changes, it became a member of the WTO in 2001, accepting harsher terms than other developing countries.[8] Exports accelerated, and the country soon became the

5. Robert S. McNamara and Brian VanDeMark, *In Retrospect: The Tragedy and Lessons of Vietnam* (New York: Times Books, 1995).

6. Xin-zhu J. Chen, "China and the US Trade Embargo, 1950–1972," *American Journal of Chinese Studies* 13, no. 2 (2006): 169–86.

7. Guangyuan Yu, Stevine I. Levine, and Ezra F. Vogel, *Deng Xiaoping Shakes the World: An Eyewitness Account of China's Party Work Conference and the Third Plenum (November–December 1978)* (Manchester: EastBridge, 2004).

8. Lee Brandsetter, "China Embraces Globalization," in *China's Great Economic Transformation* (Cambridge, UK: Cambridge University Press, 2008), 655.

"factory of the world." Anyone who visits the country today will see that it is communist in name alone. The Chinese Communist Party which once championed the working class represents the interests of all sectors of society and includes students, teachers, artists, factory managers and billionaire tycoons. In the last four decades, it has lifted over 850 million rural people out of poverty writing a new chapter in humanity's fight against poverty; China alone accounts for three-quarters of the reduction in global poverty since the 1980s and was the first developing country to meet the targets set by the United Nation's Millennium Development Goals.[9] Surveys by Pew, Gallup and Edelman show a consistently high level of trust by Chinese citizens in their government.[10] But despite these accomplishments, it faces criticism and hostility from American politicians and news media. The antipathy stems from two sources—knowledge asymmetry and ideological commitment.

Knowledge Asymmetry

In his first press conference as president, Xi Jinping declared the need for China to learn more about the world and for the world to learn more about China. Chinese parents spare no expense to have their children master English and study abroad. Never have the Chinese gone overseas in such numbers for education, and America is the favorite destination. Many Chinese professors earn their PhDs in America, and almost all theories taught in Chinese universities come from the West. Over 350,000 Chinese youths

9. "Victoria Kwakwa's Opening Speech at the China Poverty Reduction International Forum," World Bank, accessed August 25, 2020, https://doi.org/10/16/victoria-kwakwas-pening-speech-at-the-china-poverty-reduction-international-forum.

10. Weihua Chen, "Chinese Trust Government More Than Americans Do," *China Daily*, October 27, 2017.

study in America compared to some 11,000 American students in China.[11] Whereas Chinese students enroll in degree programs in America, American students usually come to China on short-term study abroad programs or study tours of two weeks to a semester to fulfill credit requirements at their home institutions. Less than 10 percent of American students enroll in undergraduate or graduate degrees in Chinese universities, and many of those are in programs where English, not Chinese, is the medium of instruction.[12] In China, Western tastes, lifestyle and values are synonymous with modernity, and the influence of Western cinema, music and fashion is everywhere to be seen. Chinese admire Western science, innovation and sports (China is the largest international market for the NBA) whereas few youths in the West can name a Chinese film, song or celebrity. The asymmetry is problematic. How we construe ourselves and the world matters because our intuition shapes our fears, impressions and relationships. Sinologist Raymond Dawson wrote that for many in the West, China is "mainly associated with such trivialities as pigtails, slant eyes, lanterns, laundries, pidgin English, chopsticks and bird's nest soup."[13] Although the "whimsical notions of a quaint civilization in a setting which resembles the design on a willow-pattern plate" have since been updated by the internet, cultural stereotypes live on. John K. Fairbank warned that

---

11. "Number of Chinese Students in the US 2019," Statista, accessed August 17, 2020, https://www.statista.com/statistics/372900/number-of-chinese-students-that-study-in-the-us/; "As Coronavirus Spreads, US Students in China Scramble to Leave," NPR.org, accessed August 17, 2020, https://www.npr.org/sections/goatsandsoda/2020/01/31/801551961/as-coronavirus-spreads-u-s-students-in-china-scramble-to-leave.

12. Joseph Stetar and Modi Li, "Is America's 100,000 Strong China Initiative Anaemic?," University World News, November 21, 2014, https://www.universityworldnews.com/post.php?story=20141120163722477.

13. Raymond Stanley Dawson, *The Legacy of China*, The Legacy Series (Oxford: Clarendon, 1964), 2.

Chinese society is very different from America, and that US policymakers would fail unless they took the difference into account. "One of our worst enemies is wishful thinking, subjectivism and sentiment. Another is plain ignorance."[14] Gone are the days of the China Hands—diplomats, journalists and soldiers with intimate knowledge of the language, culture and people of China.[15] Many were missionary kids who grew up speaking fluent Chinese but were purged from the State Department during the McCarthy era. The United States lost a generation of talented people, which has had an adverse effect on US foreign policy since. Good relations are built on trust, and it is not possible to speak of trust without understanding or empathy.

Ideological Commitment

Ronald Reagan referred to America as the "shining city upon a hill," and George W. Bush declared that America was "chosen by God and commissioned by history to be a model to the world."[16] Bush proclaimed that the defeat of Soviet Union left only one "single sustainable mode of national success: freedom, democracy and free enterprise" and that the US would take the opportunity to "extend the benefits of freedom across the globe . . . actively work to bring the hope of democracy, development, free markets, and free trade to every corner of the world."[17] Americans

---

14. John K. Fairbank, *The United States and China*, 4th ed. (Cambridge, MA: Harvard University Press, 1979), 310.

15. James R. Lilley and Jeffrey Lilley, *China Hands: Nine Decades of Adventure, Espionage, and Diplomacy in Asia* (Washington, DC: PublicAffairs, 2009).

16. Charles M. Blow, "Decline of American Exceptionalism," *The New York Times*, November 18, 2011, http://www.nytimes.com/2011/11/19/opinion/blow-decline-of-american-exceptionalism.html.

17. "The National Security Strategy of the United States of America" (The White House, September 2002).

often see themselves as an exceptional nation with a mission to spread its values around the world. Senator J. William Fulbright cautioned his countrymen that "the richer and stronger we are, the more we feel suited to the missionary task, the more indeed we consider it our duty."[18] The "shining city on a hill" champions liberal democracy and free-market fundamentalism at home and abroad. In theory, liberal democracy consists of universal suffrage (one person, one vote) in multi-party elections, while free-market fundamentalism advocates unregulated, laissez-faire capitalism. Liberal democracy appears equitable on paper, but elections can be rigged through gerrymandering and voter suppression disenfranchising large sections of the population—often the poor and underprivileged.[19] Politicians can be bought and campaign promises forgotten. Even when taken at face value, Washington has a long history of violating its own principles by subverting democratically elected governments deemed uncooperative while embracing dictators who do its bidding.[20] According to the Pew Research Center, only 17% of Americans today say they can trust Washington to do what is right "just about always" (3%) or "most of the time" (14%).[21] The share saying they can trust the government always or most of the time has not surpassed 30% since 2007. As for unbridled capitalism, there is ample evidence linking it to financial crises and extreme inequality. Pope Francis calls it "the

18. J. William Fulbright, *The Arrogance of Power* (London: J. Cape, 1967).

19. Tova Andrea Wang, *The Politics of Voter Suppression: Defending and Expanding Americans' Right to Vote* (Ithaca, NY: Cornell University Press, 2012).

20. William Blum, *Killing Hope: US Military and CIA Interventions since World War II* (Monroe, ME: Common Courage, 1995).

21. "Public Trust in Government: 1958–2019," Pew Research Center—US Politics & Policy, April 11, 2019, https://www.pewresearch.org/politics/2019/04/11/public-trust-in-government-1958–2019/.

dung of the devil."[22] Wealth captures political power, and Thomas Piketty, Joseph Stiglitz, Paul Krugman and other economists warn against the concentration of capital in the hands of a few.[23] Franklin D. Roosevelt cautioned that "government by organized money is just as dangerous as government by organized mob." Many forget that there are alternative forms of democracy and markets. Which political and economic system to adopt depends on a country's history, culture and developmental stage. To impose one particular ideology is neither democratic nor helpful.

Behind Washington's rhetoric is a commitment to hegemony. For six decades, the US has pursued a grand strategy of primacy, seeking to maintain unrivaled international hegemony. Even though the strategy brings unsustainable costs, creates security problems, and leaves the US overstretched, Washington is opposed to changing it. The grand strategy comprises military supremacy and economic openness on American terms. Constantly worrying about the collapse of the American security order, the foreign policy establishment is predisposed to the use of military force. Michael Anton, former deputy assistant for strategic communications at the National Security Council, calls it a "priesthood" which keeps the myths that underpin US hegemony.[24] Its members rarely question the wisdom of the grand strategy and regard US hegemonic leadership as axiomatically good for America and the world. America's massive power advantage perpetuates that mind-

22. Reuters, "Unbridled Capitalism Is the 'Dung of the Devil,' Says Pope Francis," *The Guardian*, July 10, 2015, https://www.theguardian.com/world/2015/jul/10/poor-must-change-new-colonialism-of-economic-order-says-pope-francis.

23. Thomas Piketty, *Capital in the Twenty-First Century* (Cambridge, MA: Harvard University Press, 2014).

24. Patrick Porter, "Why America's Grand Strategy Has Not Changed: Power, Habit, and the US Foreign Policy Establishment," *International Security* 42, no. 4 (2018): 9–46.

set, and policymakers interpret disasters such as the 9/11 terrorist attacks and the 2008 global financial crisis not as proof of a failing strategy but evidence that the US should increase its dominance.[25] China's developmental success offends Washington, which has responded with a trade war.

Trade War

Accusing China of unfair trade practices, President Trump imposed sweeping tariffs on $550 billion worth of Chinese goods in July 2018. China responded with tariffs on $185 billion of US goods.[26] Trump sought to slash the trade deficit, but the trade deficit has risen from $544 billion in 2016 to $691 billion in the twelve months ending in October 2019.[27] A trade war will not hurt China as much as Trump hopes since exports as a share of China's economy have been falling since 2008.

In 2019, exports composed 17.4% of China's GDP, and the US accounts for only 16.8% of total Chinese exports. Domestic consumption has become the biggest driver of economic growth in China contributing as much as 60.1% to the country's economic growth in 2019. Online shopping in particular will accelerate as network infrastructure and telecommunications services improve further with 5G connectivity.[28]

25. Benjamin H. Friedman and Justin Logan, "Why Washington Doesn't Debate Grand Strategy," *Strategic Studies Quarterly* 10, no. 4 (2016): 14–45.

26. "The US-China Trade War: A Timeline," China Briefing News, August 21, 2020, https://www.china-briefing.com/news/the-us-china-trade-war-a-timeline/.

27. Paul Krugman, "How Trump Lost His Trade War," *The New York Times*, December 16, 2019, https://www.nytimes.com/2019/12/16/opinion/trump-china-trade.html.

28. Jie Zhang, "Consumption Remains Biggest Contributor to Economic Growth," *China Daily*, July 30, 2019, http://www.chinadaily.com.cn/a/201907/30/

Furthermore, many Chinese exports to the US contains components from Japan, South Korea, Taiwan and Singapore. Of the $409.25 worth of parts in the Apple iPhone X, China contributes $104 or 25.4%, but the usual way of measuring exports attributes the entire $409.25 to China. Conventional trade statistics significantly inflate the value of Chinese exports.[29] Pascal Lamy, former WTO director-general, points out that if trade statistics were adjusted to reflect the actual value contributed by each country, the size of the US trade deficit with China would be cut by half.[30]

Sixty percent of Chinese exports to America consists of American brands such as Apple, Nike and Gillette. Because manufacturing is vulnerable to cost pressures and low profit margins, American firms prefer to contract Chinese factories to make the product while focusing more on design and distribution to consumers at home since most of the profits come from marketing rather than from manufacturing.[31] Predictions that the trade war will spur sourcing away from China have not materialized because the advantage China offers is no longer low labor and land costs but efficient logistics and deep prototyping capabilities which are hard to replicate.[32] Chinese tooling engineers in manufacturing

---

WS5d3fe0e0a310d83056401c6e.html.

29. Yuqing Xing, "How the iPhone Widens the US Trade Deficit with China: The Case of the iPhone X," VoxEU.org (blog), November 11, 2019, https://voxeu.org/article/how-iphone-widens-us-trade-deficit-china-0.

30. "Obsolete Way of Measuring Trade Inflates China's Trade Surplus," China Daily Europe, January 3, 2011, http://europe.chinadaily.com.cn/business/2011–01/03/content_11790607.htm.

31. Yukon Huang, Cracking the China Conundrum: Why Conventional Economic Wisdom Is Wrong (Oxford: Oxford University Press, 2017).

32. Glenn Leibowitz, "Apple CEO Tim Cook: This Is the No. 1 Reason We Make iPhones in China (It's Not What You Think)," Inc.com, December 21, 2017, https://www.inc.com/glenn-leibowitz/apple-ceo-tim-cook-this-is-number-1-reason-we-make-iphones-in-china-its-not-what-you-think.html.

hubs such as Shenzhen turn blueprints into prototypes sometimes in a matter of days.

Driven by intense domestic competition, China has moved from imitator to innovator.[33] The size of the domestic market affords important advantages when it comes to innovation. China has the world's largest fintech market where digital payments are fifty times larger than the US while Baidu, Alibaba and Tencent, its three biggest internet companies, are investing in machine learning and artificial intelligence.[34] AI is built on big data, and because of its vast number of internet users, China has caught up to the US at an unexpected pace.[35] Economies of scale allows faster recoupment of R&D and tooling expenditure which translates into cost advantage over rivals in sectors requiring heavy front-end investments such as high-speed rail, nuclear power plants, solar panels, power turbines, electric vehicles and drones. Trump sought especially to close the gap on manufactured goods, but China could only offer to buy more farm products since the US refuses to sell the manufactures that China wants. In 2018, 36% of US semiconductor sales or $75 billion came from sales to China; banning chip exports to China widens the trade deficit.[36] Contrary to Trump's

---

33. George Yip and Bruce McKern, *China's Next Strategic Advantage: From Imitation to Innovation* (Boston, MA: MIT Press, 2016).

34. Yilong Du, "Imitator to Innovator: How China Could Soon Be the World's Tech Leader," *Forbes*, September 12, 2017, https://www.forbes.com/sites/insideasia/2017/09/12/imitator-to-innovator-how-china-could-soon-be-the-worlds-tech-leader/#24687da6fb40.

35. Kai-Fu Lee, *AI Superpowers: China, Silicon Valley and the New World Order* (Boston, MA: Houghton Mifflin Harcourt, 2019), https://www.amazon.co.uk/AI-Superpowers-China-Silicon-Valley/dp/132854639X/ref=sr_1_1?keywords=lee+kai-fu&qid=1555920771&s=gateway&sr=8-1.

36. Asa Fitch and Bob Davis, "US Chip Industry Fears Long-Term Damage from China Trade Fight," *Wall Street Journal*, March 9, 2020, https://www.wsj.com/articles/chip-industry-fears-damage-china-trade-fight-11583693926.

claim, it is US importers and ultimately American consumers who will pay the tariffs even as 60% to 70% of the US population lives from paycheck to paycheck.[37]

Ravaged by the virus, the US economy will take longer to recover as a result of the politicization of the pandemic; whereas China locked down entire cities and provinces comprising hundreds of millions of people, many Americans resist curbs on individual liberty. The United States has become the epicenter of the epidemic and will not see a V-shaped recovery, but international trade will continue albeit at a slower pace because the US and China, the world's two largest economies, are too interdependent to completely decouple. There will be large-scale dislocation and hardship especially in poor communities and renewed urgency to restructure the global economy to confront the far graver threats of climate catastrophe and nuclear war.[38] The twin threats to human existence can be dealt with only through internationalist collaboration, which may not happen if Washington holds on to its grand strategy.

37. Neal Gabler, "The Secret Shame of Middle-Class Americans," *The Atlantic*, May 2016, http://www.theatlantic.com/magazine/archive/2016/05/my-secret-shame/476415/?utm_source=pocket&utm_medium=email&utm_campaign=pockethits.

38. Noam Chomsky, *Internationalism or Extinction* (London: Routledge, 2019).

6

The Reformation of Investment Professions in Response to the COVID-19 Pandemic

Mark Maxwell

Over recent centuries, important social progress has been made, including justice for the masses; voice (and vote) for those who had none; freedom of expression, movement, religion, and career choice; and vastly improved accessibility to health care. Each of these improvements has been the result of shifts in social values. Some of those shifts have come out of cataclysmic shocks, like a World War or an epidemic such as Coronavirus (which I think of as a season rather than a crisis), while others have come out of ponderous glacial shifts in cultural conscience.

It is a known truth that armies prepare for the last war. So let's attempt to look with open eyes at the shifts that are happening and are likely to happen. Some things will remain largely unchanged, while other things will change dramatically.

Let's start with what is not likely to change. There has been recent speculation in the midst of this season that valuations will change to reflect new social values that are being identified as essential and valuable. Will valuations, in the form of higher multiples, reflect new social values? While most of us would like to agree with this notion, because of its altruistic foundation, I do not believe we will see a revaluation of multiples as a result of the current system-shock. The reason is that the valuation of any security, whether bond or stock, is the market's best attempt at calculating the net present value of future cash flow. This bedrock principle of investing has survived multiple cycles and shocks over several decades, even centuries.

However, I am absolutely certain that social values will drive societal spending, which means that the revenues of companies providing goods or services that respond to social values will soar. Why? Because their sales and profitability will grow in line with societal values, the net present value of future cash flow will rise, and the stock prices of these companies will rise, reflecting the expectation of growth in revenue and earnings. If there appears to be an expansion of multiples, it is only a matter of timing, showing that the stock price is moving in anticipation of the growth in revenue and earnings. Revenue and earnings will catch up to the stock price, or the stock will fall back to its previous level. I believe the long-term multiple will remain approximately unchanged.

So, what has changed or will likely change as a result of the Coronavirus crisis from an investment perspective? In my opinion:

1. Globalization has taken a significant hit. The global village has been splintered with fences, which will not come down quickly.
2. Security concerns are going to trump other considerations for the next several years.
3. The "office" has just been redefined.

Globalization

For the past five centuries the globe has been shrinking. Explorers circumnavigated the earth, discovered the various continents, and connected them with shipping lanes. This connectivity accelerated with roads and railroads, telegraphs and telephones, and then took off with airplanes, radio and wireless cellphone connectivity. The globe truly shrank, and we moved into a global village, where no place on earth was more than a couple days travel from someone, even for middle-class citizens. And communication moved from airmail, which took weeks; to faxes, which took hours; to email, which took minutes; to shared editing for real-time word processing dialogue. Airports became as crowded as train terminals and highways. Metropolitan areas saw daily rush "hour" drag on for four hours before reversing direction.

Then came the Coronavirus crisis. Air travel was effectively banned, trains and highways emptied out, and everyone around the world was told to shelter at home or self-quarantine for their own safety as well as the welfare of others. I discovered, to my chagrin as an educator, that education was not an essential service, so we made the quick two-day transition to online education.

On the positive side, the earth has been given a rest. Pollution counts dropped. People began to live inside smaller geographic circles, and people who intruded from afar were put into a penalty box for fourteen days. The globe has re-expanded. As a believer in a creator-God, this feels a bit like an enforced global Sabbath; the whole earth is being given a season of rest. And the result is that we have a much healthier earth.

But the travel industry has changed. I expect business travel will likely drop by a large percentage (33% to 50%) as video conference calling becomes the acceptable way to conduct a large component of business. The one-meeting trip ("I'm going to New York for lunch with Holly") is going to become a video call, or it will be turned into a multi-meeting trip to justify the extra cost, inconvenience and additional time needed to make the trip. Travel is no longer a luxury or a perk of a position; it may even be an unhappy necessity of a position, and may even attract hardship pay to offset the burden.

But business travel will not go away completely, because personal relationships still matter. Personal relationships have always been a competitive advantage, and that maybe be even more so in the future because of the burden of business travel. So, when one must travel, it will likely involve multiple meetings to maximize the value of the trip. And, when one has a meeting in person, it must make a memory and build a relationship to maximize the value of the trip. The competitive advantage will tilt toward the one who can develop relationships.

By contrast, while physical travel is in decline, digital connectivity has taken off, and in that sense the global village survives and even thrives. Those companies that have been able to secure their supply chains have survived and those that have been able to expand to sell both in store and online have thrived. Companies that deliver the goods that used to be bought in malls have found new life. And the companies that deliver entertainment and communication to our computers and televisions have quickly stepped in to fill the void left by the restrictions on travel and congregating.

The changes that I believe will survive the Coronavirus are:

- Travel has permanently become even more inconvenient, costly, and cumbersome. Personal interest travel will likely see a reasonable come-back, but business travel has taken a serious blow.
- We should expect that airlines will have trouble with both revenue (fewer seats will be sold because fewer people will want to travel) and profitability (density of seating has reversed due to safe spacing requirements).
- Supply chains will be shortened. Local sources will be preferred over distant ones.

Security Concerns

Security has eclipsed all other concerns since March 15, 2020 and has become the watchword of this season. First and foremost has been health care. The term *social distancing* has become part of our daily language (in fact, it is anti-social distancing, isn't it?). Thankfully we have adopted better language, like *safe distancing* and *safe spacing*, which seems more fitting.

Healthcare Security

The directors of health services, whether locally, regionally, or nationally, have become the directors of culture and industry. For the sake of health care, they have defined which industries can continue to be open and which ones must cease doing business—and for those that can continue to be open, how they will operate. Restaurants, bars, theatres, malls, schools, and churches have been either completely closed or had their levels of activity significantly altered, all in the interest of health care security.

Supply Chain Security

For decades the cost of goods has been pushed down as manufacturing has moved to locations where the cost of labour is lowest. The manufacturing heartland of America has been largely gutted, and sweatshops have grown on the opposite side of the globe. We now enjoy good quality clothes and household goods at attractive prices, albeit on the back of near slave labour, much of it being children. So, to our shame, we rotate through whimsical fashions that have gone from years to months in length.

Now, with the Coronavirus season upon us, we have discovered the fences that have sprouted between nations of the world. These, while protecting us from the disease, have disrupted our incredibly efficient supply chain that brings the essentials of life to stores with a twenty-minute drive of our front door. Toilet paper and Tylenol are just illustrations of the "just in time" inventory system that has our shipping lanes tightly wound with goods that are scheduled to be delivered on a precise schedule, sometimes hourly, after having travelled thousands of miles from their manufacturing plant. Some of these are important structural products in our society (like healthcare products), and we are discovering that we are now dependent on other countries that may not always have our best interest at the top of their agenda.

What does this mean? No longer will low cost of manufacturing determine the location of production. The cost of bringing goods to market is the sum of manufacturing cost (raw material and labour), shipping cost (packaging, fuel, carriers, and containers), time to market, and border crossing hurdles. That formula now has an additional cost: the risk of disruption. So, we should expect that supply chains will be shortened. Buying domestic and paying more for the cost of labour will be compared with the costs of delivery from remote locations, and paying more in labour for locally produced goods may be preferred to the hidden costs of time and shipping. In addition, we should expect inventories to increase to offset the risk of another interruption in the global supply chain.

We should expect that automation of manufacturing will accelerate, which will reduce demand for sweat-shop production and may help alleviate unfair labour policies in countries that have undeveloped social consciences. At the same time, this will introduce hardship on those families that live hand-to-mouth, dependent on meagre incomes from all members of their families, including children. Those manufacturers that are at risk of losing their Western buyers may move to develop economic links or even ownership links with their buyers as a way of securing their pipeline to market.

Food Source Security

One supply chain that seems to have come through this season well is the food supply chain. It is remarkable that fresh produce is available across this continent, and even more remark-ably, it has continued to be available throughout this Coronavirus season. What has changed dramatically is the delivery. Grocery stores and pharmacies have introduced time-consuming protocols of cleaning and processing. Sanitation stations are at every store entrance, and line lengths have tripled as people are spaced out around the store, waiting patiently for their personal checkout time.

However, food scarcity has become very real for many around the world. Large portions of the poor are desperate for food and would consider food security a luxury. It would be in the best interest of every person on earth that all people enjoy food security. It would make the world a better and safer place.

As we consider the security of our food supply chain, federal governments would be wise to consider the important issue of food security for all the people in their nation. A more serious pandemic than this might have broken the food supply chain, and a hungry nation is a difficult nation to lead. It is likely that the cost of food is going up, partly to offset the higher cost of delivery, and partly to secure the supply chain against further disruptions in the future.

The changes that I believe will survive the Coronavirus are:

- Health care security has become *the* senior cabinet ap-pointment at the national level. This portfolio represents the new forefront of a nation's security.
- Companies in this industry have just been given a lift in national importance.
- We may not buy more health care services, but we will pay more for what we buy.
- Buying American will be beautiful, even if it costs a little more. Buying Canadian will be divine, if possible. The manufacturing heartland of North America will likely

see long-term recovery and will likely be accompanied with robotic ingenuity.

- Unfortunately, the countries that have been the low-cost producers will suffer from a lack of demand for their low-cost goods. Sadly, as happens too often, the poor from these countries will suffer the most.

- To offset the loss of their international buyers, we should expect these low-cost producers to establish tied relationships, probably ownership, with their buyers with clearly established and loyal commitments to their buyers.

The Office

For several decades, thought leaders have been skeptical about the value of high cost real estate in city-centres. Working from home ("WFH") was viewed as less than professional, and perhaps even the way to avoid work. The debate has become more compelling as technology has improved, allowing clear and dependable communication on the personal level, while not being widely embraced on the corporate level. In just a few months, video conferencing has become the way to visit a colleague, to collaborate on ideas and to move decisions forward. What used to be a walk down the hall for a short chat has become a quick call to explore an idea.

There are multiple benefits of this new paradigm. The commute to work is now a walk down the hall to the home office or the kitchen for a cup of coffee. The short chat in the office, now a video conference call, is no longer interrupted with multiple visits along the way. The high rent for office space in the city-centre is being replaced by the home office.

There are also some drawbacks. The human touch (and fun?) of doing business together is largely lost and hampered by distance. WFH has the inevitable interruptions of home life, like children, pets, or hobbies and other personal distractions.

Interestingly, there are early indicators of improved productivity when people are working from home with no commute, fewer disruptions, and better mind-space to focus on projects. One article speculated that a person has an extra three hours of productivity per day when working from home over a day working in the office.

To be sure, there will still need to be an executive office, and some senior people will need to be gathered there, although they may not need to be there every day. And equally certain, some people will work better in an office environment while others are more self-motivated and work better on their own. The bigger question might be, can the bosses handle not controlling the minions? Will they feel they have lost too much by not being able to see the group they command? Their egos will have to take a longer Sabbatical.

The changes that I believe will survive the Coronavirus are:

- WFH is here to stay. Companies will either figure out how to make it work, or they will lose many of their best employees who prefer working on their own—in their pajamas, on their back porches.
- Large central office space that used to command a premium in Class A high rise buildings is likely to be available in abundance, and it will fall in value. This would suggest that commercial real estate companies will go through a re-structuring, potentially quite costly, for the next several years.
- WFH'ers will likely move toward pay for production or blended fixed plus variable pay, giving partial compensation for the responsibility they carry in their firm plus the production that is needed for the success of the company.
- WFH'ers will live in nicer homes in nicer neighbourhoods, as what they used to spend on proper office attire

and on commuting is spent on a better home office and lawn care.

On the Banking, Investment Banking, and Investment Management Industries

I see no significant changes coming in the banking industry. These companies are primarily information technology companies that use technology to deliver capital and financial services. Most have continued to innovate the delivery of online banking. They are well positioned to provide financial services during this season and well into the future. If a bank has not been investing in development of online banking services, then it is at a significant disadvantage, so much so that I would expect they are vulnerable to being taken over by a stronger player. So this could be a window of opportunity for acquisition and expansion.

For many good reasons, investment banking has relied on decisions made by people who gather together in a room, therefore this will not likely become an industry in which WFH works very well. Given the size of capital involved, relationships are critical to client business decisions. Therefore, while the competitive advantage in banking is with the banks that have strong technology, a similar competitive advantage in investment banking is with the firm that has the strongest client relationships, with both corporate issuers of debt and equity, as well as with institutional investment managers who provide the funding for the corporate issuers.

There is nothing new about this. The best investment banks have solid balance sheets and great relationships. This season has simply identified new opportunities for the work of the investment bankers, who are now helping refinance the airlines, rental car companies, cruise ship companies, and hotels, as well as those companies that are stretched by the sudden demand they have enjoyed in this season (like Shopify, DocuSign, and Netflix).

The routine of in-person client meetings will likely shift from a quarterly routine to more of an annual one, with the quarterly meetings shifting to online conference calls. And we may find that senior executives take advantage of time-sharing executive jets to avoid the nuisance and irritation of public air travel. And those in-person meetings will become critical relationship building events, so I expect there will be a fair bit of thought given to turning them into "memory-maker events." For decades this has been a great industry; it is now, and it will be again.

Institutional investment management, along with the above-mentioned financial services industries, has not been seriously disrupted in this season either. Information technology is critical to being a strong player in investment management, as well as having talented professionals who have been well trained, and who are maintaining their training. And there is no training like experience. A seasoned portfolio manager, who has weathered a few "black swans" like the current COVID season, will have a distinct advantage in making good decisions about when to protect investor capital and when to put it to work. The competitive advantage among institutional investment managers will go to the firms that are led by seasoned managers, staffed by well-educated professionals, and supported by solid information technology.

Unlike investment banking, I expect WFH will become the norm in investment management. The C-suite of executives may need to go to the office more regularly (three days a week?), and the firms will continue to need good board rooms and meeting spaces, perhaps in hotels. But portfolio managers and analysts are able to work from home and collaborate with their working colleagues through video meetings. This has been possible for twenty or thirty years. The current season has simply made it obvious and accelerated the industry into this decision. I would also expect that many investment management firms will move their executive offices out of city-centres as a way of reducing costs and improving profitability.

Volatility is the friend of investors. Opportunities are presented that would not have be available without the disruption of systems and the anxiety of the general public.

Some industries have seen new levels of demand, and investors should be careful to include industries like health care and pharma/med-tech services, food services, delivery services, technology services, and agricultural services in their portfolios. There is growing interest in "ESG" (environmental, social, and governance) investing. Given the heightened focus on these issues, companies in this space will likely benefit in the wake of the COVID season, and it would not be surprising to find a few dedicated investment funds that are focused on investing in this space.

Other industries are clearly going to be restructured. Investors should use caution when including airlines and travel-related businesses (like hotels, rental car companies, and cruise lines), as well as commercial real estate companies, at least until the new habits of travel and work life are established.

Executive Summary

In short, our new investment environment and economic system is some combination of security, technology, and flexibility. Health care is probably undergoing the most significant change and will drive much of the success and failure of various industries.

I believe education will resurface as an essential service. It is not an *immediate* essential service because we can survive without education. But it is a long-term investment in a nation's economy, as well as in humanity and in culture. Investing in education is akin to making a downpayment on the future, both for the next few decades as well as for future generations.

Finally, a bit of friendly advice. Embrace change, because change is good! Welcome risk, for with it comes opportunity.

Maintain diversification. If you are a risk-taker, be sure it does not overtake you and your portfolio. Above all, practice gratitude and generosity. We live in delightful times and are enormously privileged to be having this conversation.

7

Professional Changes After the Pandemic

Samuel ("Bo") Wilson Bartholomew III

My family and I kicked off 2020 in Deer Valley, Utah. 2019 had been a brutal year of surviving a very difficult work environment while also seeing incredible growth in that company and my wife's business. We sought rest and restoration with our kids and enjoyed the beauty of the mountain and a wonderful time of rest before what would become a year unlike any other.

In the fourth quarter of 2019, we sold the company where I was a part of the C-suite. This is not the first company I have left. The idea of getting some "down time" was appealing, but inevitably I would face a difficult time during those months of transition. In *The Transforming Friendship*, Jim Houston writes, "each of us has a call from God that transcends our particular job or profession. But in the modern world, the idea of an individual 'calling' has become secularized. Our jobs have become our calling, giving us our sense of identity and our place in society." Even though I had studied vocational calling in graduate school, the identity crisis tied to corporate identification is very real and difficult. In the United States the question at any event, social gathering or family function is,

"What do you do?" Eyes would roll and shock might appear if you were to open up the conversation with, "Who are you?" The awkwardness is there when we have not sought to know who we truly are and left that question by the roadside in a hasty pursuit of crossing the finishing line of the work-life, career-oriented race that is the ethos of North America. "When will you become great again or CEO again?" was at the root of questions being asked not only by colleagues but also family members.

Entering 2020, I had read *The Second Mountain* by David Brooks. The core message of the book is how everyone pursues the top of the mountain in life—career success, ambitions, lifestyle, and the constructing of the ideal life in the pursuit of happiness—as they define it or as the world helps them define it. Yet there is a second mountain, often not discovered until you reach the peak of the first. This second mountain embodies the things that last—a vocation (well beyond an occupation), our family, our community, and our philosophy or faith. David Brooks captured these notions well by naming the first "resume virtues" and the second "eulogy virtues." The most significant difference between these two mountains is the driving motivation: serving the self is required to climb the first mountain, while serving and committing to others is required to climb the second mountain. This book was recommended to me by one of my mentors, and as the year 2020 kicked into high gear, it became the siren song calling me back when the tides of career ambition and first mountain opportunities emerged.

In January of 2020, I was fortunate to hop on a private plane with a dozen venture capitalists and head to the annual healthcare executive mecca in San Francisco, the J. P. Morgan Healthcare Conference. Every year this event attracts over 20,000 healthcare executives from around the world to share corporate strategies with analysts and to facilitate the most intense four days of networking you can imagine. Typically, I would have scheduled about forty meetings in those four days along with late night receptions and dinners to attend. This year I fell upon a free ride, a free place to stay, and no business card to declare my identity. You can imagine the number of questions when you arrive at meetings and are asked, "What do you do?," which at this event implies, "Which company are you running?" I attempted to create answers that would throw people off. "I am on sabbatical," "I am between things," "I am looking for my next company," or "I am an investor now." All of these were still tied into the career-oriented identity I was attempting not to mourn. But I felt a disorienting sensation when I could not pin myself to my job. No education, book, or counseling can prepare you to lose something you have tied your identity to. It is an emotional roller coaster with no bar holding you in.

Coming out of the conference I was prepared to jump back into the healthcare job market so I would not miss what was expected to be one of the most promising and profitable years in healthcare ever. I quickly heard from several recruiters and began the job interview gauntlet. While in pursuit of my next "calling," I found the freedom I had each day allowed me to choose who I would hang out with and be around. This became an intentional exercise for me. I sought to be around those that I thought I might like to imitate or that made me better by being around them. When you don't have a "job" that can benefit someone, you find out quickly who your true friends are. Although I won't elaborate on these friendships, it is important to know that they shaped the underlying discovery and molding process of my journey throughout the change amidst the ensuing pandemic that hit our world in 2020.

With the counsel of friends and mentors and the calling toward something greater than my own ambitions, I decided to take a course in venture capital and private equity at the Harvard Business School the first week of March 2020. My best friend, whom I've known since second grade, Brian Fox, agreed to go with me. While the course was fantastic and the curriculum and networking something special, the most memorable part was that the COVID-19 virus hit the shores in the United States while we were there. It was in Boston on the Harvard campus that we first learned about required social distancing, required hand sanitizing and the concept of quarantine that would come to define the pandemic survival methods around the world. Hospital beds were at capacity and death tolls hit all-time highs in the US.

Returning home, we discovered Boston was where the first identified cases in the US had been found. There was an onset of fear and a landslide of unanswerable questions that consumed us all. While we can all relate to the pandemic in our own way, I was simultaneously seeking the next "identity" on a business card I could call my own. Initially, Brian and I had ambitions to raise a $100 million venture fund and ride the wave so many others have before us. Once the lockdowns took effect and the markets dropped, it quickly became apparent that the timing was not right for us to raise a first-time fund. Together we had looked at eighty companies by this time in the year and found a number we could get excited about investing in or even mentoring with our operational experience.

My day to day at this point consisted of trying to figure out how to cut our losses on my wife's retail business, get out of a lease, relocate, and support four kids doing virtual school at home, managing all six of us in different rooms each day without enough internet bandwidth and WiFi. We also added a COVID puppy to our midst, so the dogs were running around each day wanting attention. I had maintained the job searches with recruiters and was attempting to interview remotely for jobs in other states. I had also picked up a few consulting clients to stay engaged in the healthcare market and to feel like I was contributing; there was pressure to provide for the family as fear of the future loomed during the pandemic.

It was in the height of the unknown—both about how our world and country would survive the pandemic and about my own vocational identity—that I found some time in solitude and in counseling with mentors. I came out of this time recognizing my deep desire for a vocation that could cure my restlessness, but also a sense of trust in the Lord who was (and is) greater than I am in figuring these things out. We all felt helpless while trying to wipe the unseen virus off our groceries and shoes. Now I felt helpless in figuring out my career-oriented calling. This helplessness forced me to turn, as we all do, to something. I found a unique peace in recognizing a higher power had better plans than I did for the future. I found that I could answer my mother's questions about what I was going to do to survive and provide with a calm assurance that I was right in the middle of my vocation already. Practically speaking I was busy with a number of consulting clients, but I began to realize what my purpose was each morning. This became crystal clear when my book group decided each of us should state our "why" at the next morning meeting in two weeks. I disclosed how uncomfortable this made me and how frightening the idea of writing down a purpose statement was when I was "between things."

When I wrote these words, the frightening world became still, and the vocational calling I have felt most of my life began to take shape. I woke up every day seeking the integrity of people, places and things, pursuing the fullness and wholeness of all things as God created them to be. This clarity awakened my soul and gave me hope when, at least from the news at the time, we lived in a world of no hope. With this backdrop I found a whiteboard and wrote down all the things that felt centered on this purpose where I could impact and help the integrity of the people, the company or the opportunity before me. I had a list of eight specific things that captured my imagination, either because of the people or because the company was a place where I could fully live out this call and use my capabilities to make a difference. Two of these were not income producing opportunities for me and my family, but they felt aligned with this newfound clarity of vocation. When I began sharing all of these, every single person said I needed to narrow these down and weed out those that were less important. Deep down, however, I felt like God was saying to pursue them all. I resolved to pursue them but recognize they may fall off as I get into them and cannot maintain a healthy set of priorities and boundaries.

While I will not go into detail on all of these, I will describe the array. One was a non-profit I was on the board of and was going to fold during the pandemic, one was a real estate investment outside my career background, and the rest were specific companies that needed investment and/or a leadership change that I could support. At the end of 2020, all eight of these opportunities had progressed and became reality for me in professional life. This required no less than a dozen board or senior leadership transitions and over $20 million of capital raised for these companies in the last eight months. At one point I found myself as CEO of two companies at the same time. Now, I am CEO of one company, on the board of several and surrounded by people I respect and love.

I have also identified a passion for the healthcare industry and invested most of my time and money on this sector that I have come to know and love. In June of this year, we were doing diligence on a healthcare technology company called EvidenceCare. The two founders were raising a Series A round and seeking our experience and investment. They shared that the founding CEO was seeking to step back and bring in an experienced executive to help take the company to the next level. What was so exciting for me was not just the role of being a CEO again and potentially shaping the culture of the company and its integrity but also how they uniquely improve the healthcare system that is broken in the US. There is so much information coming out on medical care and clinical best practice it is impossible to keep up. A physician would have to spend 160 hours a week reading the clinical studies and journals just to keep up with his specialty. Today, when a physician does not know exactly what to do with a patient and their diagnosis, 90 percent of the time they log out of their electronic medical records and go to Google searching for an answer. EvidenceCare offers an embedded software within the electronic medical records that automates that search process and populates the evidence-based protocols within doctors' workflow. Not only does this save time and help prevent physician burnout, it actually helps the hospitals collect more money because of the accuracy of documentation. The disruption our technology delivers allows the friction between the hospital providers and payers to dissipate, which in turn frees up hundreds of nurses and clinical professionals to get back to patient care and out of shuffling paperwork around, addressing denied payments and appeals to those denials. For some, this may seem mundane, but I get excited seeing our healthcare system made more efficient. When we can help hospitals make more money, doctors not get burnt out and patients to get better care, we are restoring the integrity of the health system back to what we all desire it to be. My occupation has now truly become an extension of my vocation.

During the pandemic there was documentary on the Bulls basketball team called *The Last Dance*. While watching it, I was drawn back into the locker room and the camaraderie of the difficult practices, the highs and lows of the seasons and the overcoming as a team. It was one thing for me to gain clarity on my vocation and calling, but it is another to be "in the ring" as opposed to being a spectator. The greatest part of a career change after the pandemic has been realizing that being in the game with a team is more rewarding than watching what you hope might be your perfect company or team to join. When Abby Wambach, the greatest goal scorer of all time in soccer, was asked what she missed the most, it was 100 percent her teammates, not the games, the goals, the practices or the game itself. Finding a team to be a part of and to be fully present with is as much a part of living out my profession and the alignment of it to my purpose. I am grateful for the employees and team at EvidenceCare. I am grateful to be in a company I can contribute to and apply the lessons I have learned in the past. I am grateful that we wake up every day as a company and have the chance to improve our healthcare system and bring it to a greater "fullness" or integrity, as it is meant to be.

8

A New Age of Collaboration in the Scientific Community?

Denis R. Alexander

Pandemics change millions of lives, not just those who live, suffer or die from the disease, but also those that radically change direction as either a direct or indirect consequence.

My paternal grandfather, whom I never knew, lost his life in the so-called (and incorrectly labelled) "Spanish flu" [H1N1 influenza] epidemic of 1918–1920 (Spinney, 2018). As a general practitioner he had worked as a medic all through the years of the First World War in Portsmouth, not far from its famous harbour. His two oldest sons both fought and died in the army during the War. Philip was killed in the Battle of the Somme in 1916, at the age of twenty-three; Alan, twenty-one, was shot dead in 1917 as he entered Jerusalem marching under General Allenby. My grandfather subsequently volunteered as a medical naval doctor and in 1918 was serving on the Empress of Britain as the ship brought US soldiers back to New York as the War ended. Spanish flu was rife on the ship, and my grandfather caught it while tending the sick, was subsequently hospitalised in New York, and died that December before being buried in a pauper's grave. From September to November 1918, 20,608 people died from the flu in New York, a per-capita death rate that was comparable to the COVID-19 death rate in the city during March–April, 102 years later (Faust et al., 2020).

My father was just twelve when his father died from H1N1, having lost two of his older brothers in the previous two years. Instead of his earlier aspiration to become an opera singer, he became a timber merchant. The whole direction of his life was changed, and therefore so was mine. As a young boy I enjoyed using my grandfather's medical microscope, stimulating my interest in the anatomy of the creepy-crawlies found in the pond in the back garden. Growing up, my grandfather's invisible shadow was always present.

Pandemics transform the directions of lives, and in the long term their bitter fruit can be used to transform societies and communities in positive ways. How might this principle work out in the scientific community?

Collaboration and Competition in Science

The community of modern science has always functioned as a complex mingling of collaboration and competition. Greater collaboration in recent years has been driven by the sheer scale and ambition of certain scientific projects. In 2019 the number of authors on a physics paper broke the 5,000 barrier for the first time with a total of 5,154 authors (Aad, 2015). The first nine pages of the thirty-three-page article describes the actual research, whereas the other twenty-four pages list the authors and their institutions. The collaboration was based round the use of the large Hadron Collider in Geneva.

Although this example is exceptional, having hundreds of authors on scientific papers is now not uncommon, and large international collaborations are a normal and well-accepted feature of the scientific enterprise. One of the first great international science endeavours to pave the way was the project to sequence the first human genome, the fruit of a large international collaboration led by Francis Collins over most of the project's thirteen years (1990–2003). More recently the extent of international collaborations has been measured by the journal *Nature* as part of its annual survey of the top "science cities" of the world. The survey for 2019 found two trends emerging as science globalisation accelerates: "the spread of research hubs beyond their traditional concentrations of Boston, London and Paris, and a rapid increase in international collaborations" (Csomos et al., 2020). The number of co-authored papers between academics at institutions in Beijing and New York increased from an average of fourteen per year from 1994 to 1996 to 712 per year from 2014 to 2016. A study in 2018 showed that 23% of all science papers are from authors coming from at least two countries, an increase from 13.2% in 2000 (NSB, 2019). A report by the Royal Society showed that countries engaged in international collaborations experienced more than a threefold increase in their publication citations by collaborating with one or more researchers from partner countries (Society, 2011).

When seeking to identify a large number of variant genes that contribute to the variation in a human population with regard to a medical syndrome, the only way forward is to set up a large international organisation that will nurture and support collaborations between scientists from all over the world. The Psychiatric Genomics Consortium, which involves more than 800 researchers from more than 150 institutions located in forty countries, provides a good example of such an organisation.[1]

1. https://www.med.unc.edu/pgc/, accessed September 29, 2020.

A different type of collaboration is illustrated by the NIH funded programme "All of Us,"[2] which aims to recruit one million people from diverse ethnic backgrounds in order to create a database on their clinical health in relation to their biology that will eventually benefit researchers and health providers around the world. As a health provider, the Mayo Clinic is already committed to storing 32 million samples for this programme.

When it comes to the individual research leaders in any scientific enterprise who practice a spirit of open and trusted collaboration, the data quite clearly show that their practice of collaboration leads to greater outputs and indeed greater success in their own scientific careers. For example, one study analysed 1.25 million science papers published between 1996 to 2012 in eight different disciplines and found that international collaborations led to publications in higher ranked journals that were then cited more frequently (Smith et al., 2014). A key element in making the collaboration work well is trust (Bennett and Gadlin, 2012). It is perhaps not surprising that the Wellcome Trust based in the UK funded a programme from 2017–2019 called "Together Science Can," which had the specific aim "to champion international science collaboration through online community building and grassroots activism."[3]

Collaborations at the level of the individual laboratory, rather than at the institutional level, work best when they emerge from informal interactions that occur during international conferences, or when visiting another institution to give a seminar. There is no "magic formula" for an effective collaboration, but there are several key factors that can impede collaboration. One recent study surveyed 9,422 biologists and physicists in eight

2. https://allofus.nih.gov, accessed September 29, 2020.

3. https://medium.com/together-science-can/about-together-science-can-264b3b4e8e1f, accessed September 30, 2020.

countries and regions—the United States, the United Kingdom, India, Italy, Taiwan, Hong Kong, Turkey, and France, to determine the most important factors that impede collaborations (Matthews et al., 2020). Funding was universally the chief concern in each society surveyed. Scientists also noted issues such as material and data sharing regulation, and difference in academic standards, as prominent obstacles. In addition, scientists described perceived biases against scholars in emerging and developing countries. The great majority of respondents in the areas studied judged international collaboration to be of importance, more than 90 percent of respondents in the case of Italy, Hong Kong and Turkey.

The level of collaboration between different research groups around the world is remarkable when one considers that the scientific enterprise also operates through competition. The race to be the first to publish a key new discovery in a top scientific journal such as *Nature* or *Science* can be intense. A career may make or break if the early career scientist who is first author on the paper manages to publish in such a top journal. Most curious (and challenging) of all is the fact that submitted papers are very often reviewed by your competitors. Not only do the reviewers have the opportunity to read your results prior to publication, but they also have the power to block publication in a top journal by being overly critical of your paper. There are countless examples in the community of ground-breaking discoveries that never made it into the top journals because of blocks put in the way by rival researchers who perhaps held to a different theory to explain the results. The so-called "Invisible College" still operates within the international scientific community, who act as gate-keepers. The term has been used historically with various nuances, for example to refer to particular groups within the early Royal Society. But the term can be used to refer to the leaders of a particular research area within a particular discipline. Everyone in that particular research area knows who these people are, and it is they who tend to control who is invited to speak at top international conferences and what papers in that field gain entry into the best journals. I once had a post-doc in my laboratory who presented her results at an international conference and was told very firmly by one of the leaders of the field who was organising that conference that there was no hope that her work would be published in a top journal unless he had personally given the work his green light.

So given this background, it is interesting to see how the COVID-19 pandemic has been helping to shift the balance between collaboration and competition.

The COVID-19 Effect on Collaboration

From the beginning of the COVID-19 pandemic, it has been clear that effective international collaborations would help the scientific biomedical community to tackle the viral blaze more effectively. The comments posted on the website of Charles River, a major biomedical research agency based in the USA, are typical: "Finding effective treatments for COVID-19 is a team effort. It takes collaboration and harmony from many stakeholders to get a therapy in the hands of those who need it quickly."[4]

A pioneering initiative that well illustrates this point is the ACTIV public-private partnership initiated by the National Institutes of Health [NIH] in April 2020 to bring together government, industry and non-profit agencies in coordinated efforts to tackle the pandemic.[5] Co-chaired by NIH Director Francis Collins and Paul Stoffels, CSO of Johnson and Johnson, ACTIV has four fast-track working groups to accelerate progress: the identification of preclinical treatments; the clinical testing of the most promising vaccines and treatments; clinical trial impact and effectiveness;

4. https://www.criver.com/insights/collaborating-towards-cure-COVID-19?region=3696.

5. https://www.nih.gov/research-training/medical-research-initiatives/activ.

and regulatory requirements of new treatments. In reflecting two months after its formation on how ACTIV could have made such rapid progress, Collins commented that "one key factor that helped to speed the formation of this partnership was having the US and European government regulatory agencies directly involved from the outset" (Collins and Stoffels, 2020). As Collins and Stoffels point out, ACTIV's partners have embraced the spirit of a principle attributed to President Harry S. Truman: "It is amazing what you can accomplish if you do not care who gets the credit."

Vaccines

Within the scientific community, a striking and early example of the principle of collaboration was the open online publication on January 10, 2020 of the genome sequence of the SARS-CoV-2 (severe acute respiratory syndrome coronavirus 2)[6] RNA virus, which causes COVID-19, by researchers in China and Australia (Wu et al., 2020). This immediately provided the key data required to start making a vaccine by any group or company in the world, at least for vaccines that require the genomic sequence for their generation method. "We were making RNA within a week or so" of the SARS-CoV-2 sequence being published, said Drew Weissman, who researches RNA vaccines at the University of Pennsylvania Perelman School of Medicine (Abbasi, 2020b). The publication of the sequence led to the first initial tests for a possible vaccine just sixty-six days after its online publication.

Hundreds of researchers worked on potential vaccines against COVID-19 around the world and dozens went to clinical trials. Of interest here are the ways in which the urgent search for a good vaccine has stimulated some striking examples of scientific collaboration. For example, during the first peak of the epidemic in April 2020, the "Access to COVID-19 Tools" (ACT) Acceler-

---

6. Severe acute respiratory syndrome coronavirus 2.

ator was established as a ground-breaking global collaboration to accelerate development, production, and equitable access to COVID-19 tests, treatments, and vaccines. The ACT Accelerator brings together a wide range of governments, scientists, businesses, civil society, philanthropists and global health organizations. These organizations joined forces to speed up an end to the pandemic by supporting the development and equitable distribution of the tests, treatments and vaccines the world needs to reduce mortality and severe disease, restoring full societal and economic activity globally in the near term, and facilitating high-level control of COVID-19 disease in the medium term.[7]

COVAX is that section of the ACT Accelerator which focuses on vaccine development and distribution. A global initiative, it works with governments and manufacturers to ensure COVID-19 vaccines are available worldwide to both higher-income and lower-income countries. By August 2020, 172 countries had committed to the COVAX programme,[8] which is co-led by the Coalition for Epidemic Preparedness Innovations (CEPI), Gavi, the Vaccine Alliance, and the World Health Organization (WHO)—working in partnership with developed and developing country vaccine manufacturers. COVAX represents the main global initiative that is working with governments and manufacturers to ensure COVID-19 vaccines are available worldwide to both higher-income and lower-income countries. As Richard Hatchett, CEO of CEPI, has commented: "In the scramble for a vaccine, countries can act alone—creating a few winners, and many losers—or they can come together to participate in COVAX, an initiative which is

7. This description is quoted from the WHO website: https://www.who.int/initiatives/act-accelerator. Accessed October 2, 2020.

8. https://www.who.int/news-room/detail/24-08-2020-172-countries-and-multiple-candidate-vaccines-engaged-in-COVID-19-vaccine-global-access-facility, accessed October 2, 2020.

built on enlightened self-interest but also equity, leaving no country behind."

The COVAX Facility is coordinated by Gavi, the Vaccine Alliance, which itself well illustrates the power of partnership. Gavi was originally set up in 2000 as a public-private global health partnership with the goal of increasing access to immunisation in poor countries. Gavi's impact draws on the strengths of its core partners, the World Health Organization, UNICEF, the World Bank and the Bill & Melinda Gates Foundation, and plays a critical role in strengthening primary health care in order to make it universally available. The COVID-19 pandemic has highlighted the critical role played by international organisations such as Gavi.

In this context it also needs to be mentioned that during 2020 the US withdrew from supporting the WHO and, partly for that reason, also then withdrew from collaboration with COVAX.[9] This was for political reasons and illustrates the difficulties experienced by the international scientific community on occasion when collaborative efforts are hindered for such reasons.

The challenge for commercial companies to collaborate in vaccine production is somewhat more complicated due to patents, data security and responsibilities to share-holders. Nevertheless the pandemic has stimulated some welcome collaborations between companies. Early on as the pandemic began to sweep the world, Sanofi and GSK, two huge pharmaceutical companies, announced a joint collaboration to develop a COVID-19 vaccine. Paul Hudson, chief executive officer of Sanofi, said in announcing the collaboration: "As the world faces this unprecedented global

9. https://www.washingtonpost.com/world/coronavirus-vaccine-trump/2020/09/01/b44b42be-e965–11ea-bf44–0d31c85838a5_story.html, accessed October 8, 2020.

health crisis, it is clear that no one company can go it alone."[10] Collaborations between companies and academic research laboratories have of course helped to drive scientific discoveries for many years, but again the pandemic has helped to stimulate many more. A further major collaboration with the aim of generating a vaccine was announced at the end of April 2020 between the Jenner Institute and the Oxford Vaccine Group together with AstraZeneca, another large pharmaceutical company.[11]

The Jenner Institute is named after Edward Jenner, one of the first physicians to introduce a vaccine for smallpox, when he infected a young boy with cowpox in 1796. Prior to that time the use of inoculation was widespread—involving the introduction of the smallpox virus itself under the skin. Vaccination was different because the material used came from cows (Latin *vacca,* cow), and Jenner obtained his material from a young dairy-maid who had fresh cowpox lesions on her hands and arms. In the eighteenth century in Europe, on average 400,000 people died from smallpox every year, and of those who survived, one-third went blind (Barquet and Domingo, 1997). Today the disease has been eradicated, thanks in no small part to Jenner's pioneering work and those who followed in his footsteps.[12] Jenner, son of an Anglican clergyman, had himself been inoculated against smallpox

10. https://pharmanewsintel.com/news/sanofi-gsk-partner-to-develop-adjuvanted-COVID-19-vaccine, accessed October 2, 2020.

11. https://www.astrazeneca.com/media-centre/press-releases/2020/astrazeneca-and-oxford-university-announce-landmark-agreement-for-COVID-19-vaccine.html, accessed October 2, 2020.

12. It may well have been the case that Benjamin Jesty was actually the first to vaccinate against smallpox shortly before Jenner (P. J. Pead, *Benjamin Jesty: New Light in the Dawn of Vaccination,* Lancet 362 [2003]: 2104–9). But as Riedel comments: "It was Jenner's relentless promotion and devoted research of vaccination that changed the way medicine was practiced" S. Riedel, *Edward Jenner and the History of Smallpox and Vaccination,* Proc. 18 (2005): 21–25.

in 1757 as an eight-year-old boy (Riedel, 2005). Later he became a respected naturalist, scientist and physician, being elected to the Royal Society due to his pioneering study to understand cuckoo behaviour. His pioneering work on vaccination came from his own determination to persuade his critics that some solid experimental science supported vaccination, and by the early 1800s Jenner was receiving widespread honours and recognition for his work. Jenner saw his scientific work as a way of understanding the works of God in creation. As he wrote to his friend Thomas Pruen: "The weather may be inconvenient for the designs of man, but must always be in harmony with the designs of God, who has not only this planet, our Earth, to manage, but the universe. The whole creation is the work of God's hands. It cannot manage itself. Man cannot manage it, therefore, God is the manager" (Drewitt, 1931). As Jenner observed to an intimate friend not long before his death, he wondered not that the people were ungrateful to him for his discovery, but he was surprised that they were ungrateful to God for the benefits of which he was the humble means.[13]

Jenner believed in good science, vigorous communication, friendly collaboration and a determined spirit in the face of opposition and misunderstanding. It is the same kind of spirit that today will see good COVID-19 vaccines available to the poorest parts of the world, vaccines that have received careful and systematic scientific assessment.

The Science of Therapeutics

The COVID-19 pandemic has stimulated many new initiatives in the search for effective therapeutics and some important scientific collaborations have been pushing the work forward at

---

13. https://www.gjenvick.com/Biography/EdwardJenner/1894-DrEdward-Jenner--Smallpox-Physician.html#sthash.15vtDKHE.dpbs, accessed October 2, 2020.

breakneck speed. Intellectual property [IP] barriers can provide a hindrance to the rapid achievement of collaborative goals. It was therefore significant that the Open COVID Pledge was established in April 2020, which enables organisations to make their IP widely available without charge.[14] Later in the year the Creative Commons took on the leadership and stewardship of the Pledge, which now covers more than 250,000 patents worldwide (Contreras et al., 2020).

Once again scientists have led the way in collaborating on the science that in turn will lead to new therapeutics. As soon as the SARS-CoV-2 RNA virus sequence became available in January 2020, a global network of biologists interested in the structure of viral proteins set to work (Editorial, 2020). As the journal *Nature* reports, "The network included the Center for Structural Genomics of Infectious Diseases, a consortium of 40 scientists across 8 institutions in the United States and Canada, which played a central part in the project." Within a few months, partial or complete structures of SARS-CoV-2 viral proteins had been worked out, revealing binding sites for possible drugs to treat COVID-19. At the same time, structural biologists at Shanghai Tech University in China began the task of revealing the structure of a key enzyme that the virus needs to replicate. The team deposited its results in the Protein Data Bank[15]—an open-access digital repository for 3D biological structures—available for researchers around the world to access. As they worked, Shanghai team members collaborated with structural biologists at the University of Oxford to share knowledge and avoid overlap (Editorial, 2020).

Drug discovery flourishes when a strong collaborative aspect is present. A dream for every new infectious disease that appears is to identify drugs already in use for other conditions that might

14. https://openCOVIDpledge.org/about/.
15. https://www.rcsb.org.

also combat the new one. The reasons are obvious: the drug will already have passed all its clinical safety tests and it will be sitting on the shelf "ready to go." Imagine the delight when it was discovered that the well-known anti-inflammatory drug dexamethasone was able to ameliorate COVID-19 symptoms, especially in patients with severe disease (Group et al., 2020; Cain and Cidlowski, 2020). Many collaborations are under way to rapidly screen a large number of existing reagents to find the "next dexamethasone."

What might hopefully linger after the pandemic is the culture of collaboration across government, industry and academia that has emerged during the outbreak (Ledford, 2020). The pandemic has touched nearly all aspects of the industry, comments Kenneth Kaitin, director of the Tufts Center for the Study of Drug Development in Boston. "This has really turned upside down the whole drug-development process." And as Esther Krofah, executive director of Faster Cures, a Washington, DC think tank, comments: "We have traditional competitors working together in new ways. An alliance of more than a dozen companies . . . has been working to discover and test antiviral treatments by sharing data about early results and basic science, as well as collaborating on designs for clinical trials" (Ledford, 2020).

Collaborative People in the Right Place at the Right Time

In reflecting on the many different ways in which the COVID-19 pandemic has stimulated collaboration and cooperation between many different people and organisations—and the examples given above are but the tip of a large iceberg—one striking observation is the way in which God has placed key people in key positions with the gifts and experience to help make such collaborations actually happen.

One striking example is Francis Collins, NIH Director, who has made no secret of his active Christian faith.[16] Collins became well-known during his years as Director of the National Human Genome Research Institute for not only coordinating the great international scientific collaboration to sequence the human genome, but also for effectively bringing together gifted scientists to accomplish the task who would never normally work together but for his wise and reconciling leadership. It was Francis Collins whose leadership of the NIH at such a critical time in its history led to the ACTIV collaboration already described. In 2020 Francis Collins was awarded the Templeton Prize, an award that was decided long before the COVID-19 pandemic came on the scene. In retrospect the timing of the award could not have been better; it provided providential opportunities to highlight not only the importance of science in tackling the epidemic, but also the importance of his Christian faith in how he practiced science. Collins titled his acceptance speech at the Templeton Prize ceremony "In praise of harmony."[17] Personally I am reminded of that remarkable message from Mordecai to Esther in the Old Testament: "And who knows but that you have come to royal position for such a time as this?" (Esther 4:14). Being NIH Director is certainly not a royal position! But the principle remains the same: God has his people in the right place at the right time in order to accomplish his purposes.

I was reminded likewise of that principle when reading an interview with Anthony Fauci who has served as the director of the National Institute of Allergy and Infectious Diseases in the USA since 1984. Dr Fauci has become well-known for his measured and unruffled attitudes and responses, even within the highly intense atmosphere often created by the pandemic. Dr Fauci was asked

16. Francis Collins describes his pathway from atheism to faith in Christ in his best-selling book *The Language of God* (New York: Simon & Schuster, 2007).

17. https://www.youtube.com/watch?v=hL6Ua8nXR7Y&t=32s.

how he maintains such calm in the midst of such situations and responded by saying: "I went to a Jesuit high school in Manhattan, and from there I went to a Jesuit college. I think it was just right for me because I had always been interested in public service and not being somebody that ever attacks anybody, that accepts them for who they are and what they are. So it was kind of the perfect atmosphere to me to be educated in, and I just carried it along with me" (Abbasi, 2020a).

There are without doubt many others around the world within the scientific community who have been playing heroic and often unsung roles in the midst of the pandemic, practicing collaboration and harmony in the midst of stress and sometimes harsh and unjustified criticism.

Christian Values in the Practice of Science

It is no exaggeration to say that the scientific community is an important preserver of Christian values. That may sound surprising to some who think that in some way religion is "anti-science." Nothing could be further from the truth. The emergence of modern science in the sixteenth and seventeenth centuries was shaped and nurtured by its theological roots. The founders of the Royal Society in England consisted mainly of Christian believers, many of whom understood the goal of the scientific enterprise as the uncovering of the works of God's creation. The 1663 charter declares that its activities shall be devoted "to the glory of God the Creator, and the advantage of the human race," and its officers were required to swear an oath on "the holy Gospels of God." Thomas Sprat, the Society's first historian, noted that the experimental study of nature was really a form of religious worship.

Therefore aspirational Christian values were part and parcel of the modern scientific enterprise from the beginning, even though it has to be said that some of the early Fellows of the Royal Society were not particularly collaborative, Sir Isaac Newton providing a notorious example. Neither are those aspirational values necessarily practiced by all scientists today even though all would probably acknowledge collaboration as being a worthy ideal aim. As the historian Tom Holland points out, the influence of the teachings of Jesus has been so deep and profound over the past 2,000 years that many secular thinkers do not realise, or perhaps wish to admit, the source of their value systems (Holland, 2019). But without those values being maintained by the great majority, the scientific enterprise would collapse, and the pandemic has further highlighted their importance.

Here just three key values will be mentioned to illustrate this point, although the list in reality is far longer than this.

Truth-Telling

It may seem obvious that scientists need to tell the truth about their science, but this became critical as empiricism began to play a central role during the emergence of modern science. Modern science began to flourish within a theistic worldview in which curiosity-driven research was driven by a desire to find out how God's universe actually worked. Since God was deemed to be the source of all truth, and everything that existed was created and sustained by his ongoing activity, a central goal of the scientific enterprise was to engage in truth-telling about God's creative actions. The motivation for truth-telling was underpinned by a particular theological worldview.

Today in many situations a head of lab needs to sign the lab notebooks of those scientists in the lab who have been carrying out experiments and recording their results that day. The signature is an affirmation that the head of lab was present on the day and a witness to the fact that the researcher had obtained those particular results. This routine procedure may prove to be of critical importance in a patent application that may be made months or years later. Priority of discovery may also depend on what is written. It is the duty of every researcher to make an accurate record of the experimental protocol and the results obtained.

The importance of truth-telling in science helps to explain why episodes of fraud, which do happen occasionally, are treated with such alarm and despondency within the scientific community. From a pragmatic perspective, false results can waste years of work by another researcher in the field, as they may base their whole enquiry on what has (apparently) been discovered by another scientist. Fraudulent practices, often accompanied by mass media exposure in high-profile cases, can lead to an understandable and possibly damaging loss of trust by the general public in the vast majority of scientific findings that remain trustworthy and well-authenticated.

In 1998 the now discredited British physician Andrew Wakefield published a paper in the medical journal *The Lancet* claiming that the measles, mumps and rubella [MMR] vaccine was a cause of autism. Other researchers were unable to reproduce Wakefield's findings, and most of his co-authors then withdrew their support for the interpretation of his findings. *The Lancet* formally retracted Wakefield's paper on February 2, 2010. Despite being found "dishonest and irresponsible" in his autism research by the British General Medical Council and losing his medical licence to practice as a doctor in Britain, Wakefield then moved to the US to continue his anti-vaccination campaigning. Wakefield's false claims of a link between MMR vaccination and autism was almost certainly one of the factors that led to a reduction in measles vaccination levels in many countries with consequent outbreaks of measles and loss of life.[18] According to the WHO, measles killed an estimated 141,000

18. Merrit Kennedy, "Samoa Arrests Anti-Vaccination Activist as Measles Death Toll Rises," NPR News, http://www.npr.org/2019/12/06/785487606/samoa-arrests-anti-vaccination-activist-asmeasles-death-toll-rises, accessed October 3, 2020.

people during 2018, most of them children under the age of five, deaths that vaccination could readily have prevented.

Telling the truth in science really does matter—lives are at stake. The COVID-19 pandemic has highlighted the ongoing anti-vaccination campaigns, which are often based on fake news spread via social media (Johnson et al., 2020). Making vaccination a political issue of some kind is also unhelpful. The percentage of Americans who say they would get vaccinated for COVID-19 fell from 72% in May 2020 to 51% in September the same year.[19] Such findings are important because vaccination is a community project. Those involved in the collaborations that generate and distribute good vaccines are only too aware of the need to be completely open about the clinical trials and their results. Truth-telling increases confidence and undermines fake news.

Unfortunately, the COVID-19 pandemic has not only led to some truly remarkable and well-researched biomedical publications but also to many thousands of papers being submitted for publication that are simply "riding the band-wagon" in an attempt to publish shoddy work. The editor of a well-known scientific journal shared with me that while hundreds of papers are currently being received with "COVID" in the title, at least 90 percent are editorially rejected for publication on the grounds that they are insufficiently rigorous or are just using the COVID label to present results about something rather different. There is an increasingly large collection of retracted papers on COVID-19 on the website Retractionwatch.[20]

Telling the truth is a consistent and central theme in the Biblical record. The Old Testament book of Proverbs provides many examples: "The LORD detests lying lips, but he delights in men who

---

19. https://www.pewresearch.org/science/2020/09/17/u-s-public-now-divided-over-whether-to-get-COVID-19-vaccine/, accessed October 3, 2020.

20. https://retractionwatch.com/retracted-coronavirus-COVID-19-papers/.

are truthful" (Prov. 12:22); "a truthful witness does not deceive, but a false witness pours out lies" (Prov. 14:5) Again and again in the Gospel records, Jesus assures his listeners that "I tell you the truth."[21] The principle of truth-telling is likewise central to the flourishing of the scientific enterprise.

Trust

Trust is based on truth-telling. Scientists will often remark that they believe some new results "because they came out of Prof. X's lab," and they just know they can trust those results because Prof. X is well-known as a careful investigator in the field who does not rush out their results for publication before s/he is quite sure that they are well justified. The converse is equally the case.

The historian Steven Shapin points out how the early Royal Society, with its motto *Nullius in verba* ("take no one's word for it"), came to equate trustworthiness with gentlemanly origins. As Shapin has pointed out, early scientists like Robert Boyle were listened to precisely because of their social status. A gentleman was held to be competent in describing sensory experiences; had to tell the truth in order to preserve his social reputation; was a Christian; and was deemed to be a disinterested and financially independent observer who had no interest in personal gain from his observations (Shapin, 1994). Today the precise criteria for being trustworthy are surely different! The scientific community (in most countries) is a meritocracy in which trust is based on reputation and personal experience, but the central role that trust plays in the scientific enterprise remains the same.

Not only is trust of other scientists critical if fruitful collaborations are to endure, but trust in science and scientists by the general public is also of vital importance at all times, especially during a pandemic. Once science is misused for political or ideo-

21. For example: Matthew 5:18, 26; 6: 2,5, 16; and in many other passages.

logical advantage in society, then trust in science tends to decline, and the COVID-19 pandemic has provided countless examples of such misuse. As already noted, trust is also a key element in building effective collaborations. One reason that Francis Collins is so effective at building collaborations between a broad diversity of individuals and organisations is because they trust him—a trust based on decades of reputation and personal experience.

Above everything else, trust in God is the key to wisdom and guidance in the midst of the challenges of life. Once again the book of Proverbs puts the point very succinctly: "Trust in the Lord with all your heart and lean not on your own understanding; in all your ways acknowledge him, and he will make your paths straight" (Prov. 3:5–6).

Cooperation

Truth-telling and trust are both key elements for effective cooperation. Examples have already been given of increased international collaborations between the scientific community and other stakeholders, be it business or government agencies. A century ago the stereotypical image of the scientist all on their own in their laboratory making great break-throughs was often not far from reality. But today that is no longer usually the case, and researchers find themselves embedded in a large community where in many cases their immediate colleagues may come from a wide range of countries.

That spirit of cooperation and collaboration has deep historical roots. The Royal Society was always seen as a society of leading natural philosophers who would communicate their results with the world of learning and in turn hear what the rest of the world had to offer. The founding of the *Philosophical Transactions* in 1665, the world's oldest continuously running journal, projected the collective enterprise of science right from the beginning.[22] The post of Foreign Secretary of the Royal Society was instituted in 1723, nearly sixty years before the British Government appointed its first Secretary of State for Foreign Affairs. With its roots in a strongly Christian ethos, the Society has always looked outwards to the world as well as inwards to its own Fellows for scientific inspiration and information, though it was not really until the twentieth century that collaborative international science became a common feature of scientific research.

Certainly there is a wealth of biblical resources of the kind that inspired the early Royal Society that make clear that collaboration is greatly valued in the sight of God, that unity is far more valued than disunity, and that tolerating issues of secondary importance is critical in achieving united goals. One of the heart-felt prayers of Jesus was that his followers for all time might practice unity: "I pray also for those who will believe in me through their message, that all of them may be one, Father, just as you are in me and I am in you" (John 17:20). For the first time ever, the way of Jesus provided a faith that was open and transforming to anyone who believes from whatever background (John 5:24; 10:9). The early followers of Jesus were "together and had everything in common" (Acts 2:44). The very first church council at Jerusalem provides an early model as to how disputes should be resolved and effective collaborations built by focusing on the most important aspects of the Christian message and by putting to one side those issues of lesser importance that are causing disputes (Acts 15:5–31). The point is not that the church ever since these early days has always practiced the teaching of Jesus—far from it—nor is the point here that the scientific community, a complex mixture of those

22. As emphasised by previous President of the Royal Society, Paul Nurse, https://royalsociety.org/~/media/publishing350/publishing350-exhibition-catalogue.pdf.

of any faith or none, should be expected suddenly to behave as Jesus taught. The point, rather, is that here we have an example of the kind of principles that underlie a worldwide collaborative enterprise that has made a huge impact on the world, not least in nurturing the emergence of modern science. It is an example to follow.

Conclusions

The COVID-19 pandemic's bitter toll has led to much suffering and a change of direction in millions of lives. Yet at the same time the pandemic has stimulated new scientific collaborations that are unlikely to have happened without it. Labs, institutions and businesses that may have never thought of working together before, have now experienced unity in facing a common challenge in some new collaborative project. The benefits of working together in generating fruitful outcomes have been demonstrated time and time again. Could it not be that such collaborations will become increasingly the norm rather than the exception and, looking back a decade later, the pandemic with all its associated suffering will at the same time be seen as a key influence in having highlighted the benefits of collaboration over competition in the scientific enterprise?[23]

23. I am grateful to Prof. Bob White FRS and Prof. Keith Fox for making helpful comments on an earlier version of this chapter.

9

How to Forge a Brighter Future

Entrepreneurship in a Post-Pandemic World

Anson Kung

I remember vividly the day the pandemic became a reality for me. It was the second week of March, the fateful year of 2020. My business partner and I had been working on a new business called Oco Meals, and we had just launched the previous week.

In a dimly-lit basement suite that we were renting as an office in Vancouver, Canada, we huddled around a computer screen, waiting for the Prime Minister of Canada, Justin Trudeau, to address the nation in a hastily announced press event. Over thirty minutes past the appointed time of the address, Justin Trudeau finally appeared. It was in this address that the severity of what was to come finally hit home. With the announcement of a nationwide closure of many businesses, the grounding of all non-essential travel, the closing of borders that I never thought could close, and the call for all Canadians abroad to come home, we realized that the world as we knew it had suddenly changed.

As a technology entrepreneur starting a new business in the midst of a global pandemic, I had a front row seat as I saw and experienced first hand how it affected the world of tech entrepreneurship. In the following pages, I wish to share my experiences on how COVID has rocked the entrepreneurship world, how this sector is rising to the challenge, and how the events of today will forever shape entrepreneurship in a post pandemic world.

Nowhere did I experience the effects of COVID on entrepreneurship more acutely than in our participation with Y Combinator. Just prior to Trudeau's national address about the pandemic, my business partner Kenton and I had sent in an application to Y Combinator, a seed money start-up accelerator. Most people have not heard of it, but within the circles of tech entrepreneurship, Y Combinator—known colloquially as YC—is afforded the equivalent prestige of organizations like Harvard, MIT, and Oxford, which it earned through its track record of launching massive successes such as Dropbox, Airbnb, and Stripe. We were utterly ecstatic when we received an email from YC stating that they found our application promising and would like to invite us for an interview.

The YC interview process is infamous for the way it's run. Every company that makes it to the interview stage is flown from wherever they are in the world to San Francisco to participate in a ten-minute interview. That's right, a ten-minute interview. You are asked very direct questions about your business, and you have ten minutes to convince them that you are the best person in the world to do whatever it is you're pitching. We were looking forward to the experience of being flown to Silicon Valley, meeting and mingling with all the other entrepreneurs, and being interviewed by tech legends, while socializing and making new friends in the evening.

But alas, it was not meant to be, for COVID had come, and it was announced that the interview would be remote. Our hearts dropped upon receiving such news, knowing that the entire YC interview experience would be reduced to a ten-minute Zoom call. This was the first sting of COVID on my life as an entrepreneur.

Fortune would have it that our YC interviewers found us favourable and officially invited us to take part in YC's summer batch of 2020. This news took us to an emotional high, and we spent the weekend celebrating. We were like children looking forward to attending summer camp for the first time. We had heard stories of the YC experience. For three months, my partner and I would move down to Mountain View, California. Every week, we would attend talks, mentoring sessions, and boot camps led by some of the most famous people in the world of tech entrepreneurship. We'd get to explore a new city, attend networking events, forge new friendships, and at the end of 3 months, be put on one of the most important stages in Silicon Valley, where we'd have the opportunity to pitch to over a thousand top investors. It was everything that an entrepreneur could hope for.

But then COVID struck again. The pandemic began to spiral out of control, cases climbed, restrictions were tightened, and the world did not go back to normal the way we hoped. The news reaches us that YC summer batch 2020 will, for the very first time in history, be remote.

As the program start date approached, we were notified that every session would be held over Zoom. We wondered how this would play out. A cloud of uncertainty hung over our heads.

Come kickoff day, we were all invited to join a Zoom call. As I joined the call, I could see over two hundred other participants, pages and pages of faces on my screen. As Michael Seibel—the CEO of YC—gave his opening remarks, I could sense the familiar air of excitement and anticipation that one feels in a stadium before a sporting match or concert. It was strange to feel this way given the fact that I was sitting at home at my dining table, participating from thousands of kilometers away. It began to dawn on me that perhaps, just maybe, we didn't need to be in person to have an amazing experience.

As YCs first ever remote batch began to start, some strange things began to happen. Now keep in mind, that this is not my first time participating in an accelerator program. As a serial entrepreneur with several past ventures under my belt, I've had the opportunity to be involved in accelerators such as UBC's Lean LaunchPad, the Creative Destruction Lab, SFU venture labs, and other startup groups. In every program that I've been involved with, it's always been fun to get to know the other entrepreneurs that are on a similar journey as you. When you're in the same room, you'd say hi and strike up a short conversation. But overall it was all mostly quite surface-level. We chatted because it was the polite thing to do, and we were also curious to get to know what other people were working on. It was rare to intentionally reach out to people you haven't yet met and book coffee chats with them.

But what was strange about the program being remote was that everyone was extra intentional about getting to know others. We knew it wasn't possible to bump into them in the hallways, or sit next to them over dinner, or chat with them after attending a presentation together. But as humans, we longed for that connection. We wanted to have the interpersonal connections that we knew we would build if we had all been in person together.

So people started reaching out in many different ways. I myself posted on an internal forum, saying that it was my goal to get to know at least twenty people by the end of this program. If someone would like to connect, I invited them to shoot me an email and schedule a Zoom call.

I was far from alone in these efforts. Almost everyone took it upon themselves to be extra intentional in this age of social isolation and reach out to their fellow batchmates, people they had never met before.

The organic demand was so high that within a week or two of the program starting, somebody installed an app in our Slack chat called Donut. Donut would help automate the process of connecting with people that you had not known before. Every week, Donut would introduce you to two people that you had not yet met before. It would automatically look at both of your calendars, find several meeting times that would work for the both of you, and propose them. All you had to do was press one button, and a calendar meeting event complete with Zoom link would be automatically created for the both of you. Technology tools like this reduced the friction of meeting new people so much that I would say that it was even easier than setting up meetings in-person.

It is ironic that in a pre-COVID world, where connecting with people in-person was so easy, that we took it for granted. In the past, I knew that I would bump into others sometime in the near future, and so there was never a sense of urgency. It was something that you could so easily delay and then eventually forget about it. But now that the ease of connecting in-person has been taken away from us, we value human connection that much more, as I have observed first hand for myself and my fellow batchmates.

Another unexpected consequence of the pandemic was that it made YC more accessible to the international community. That's right, a global pandemic that has grounded air travel, closed numerous borders, and forced people to stay at home has made an entrepreneurial program located in San Francisco more accessible to people around the world. How can this be?

In the pre-COVID era, the norms of business were highly preferential to in-person interactions. The expectation was that to participate in YC, you would move to San Francisco for the full three months. This was based on the common-sense understanding that an in-person experience was the most effective and therefore led to the greatest odds of success. Obviously, this requirement made the program less accessible to people who did not already live in the SF bay area or who for whatever reason were unable to move to SF for the three-month period of the program.

By restricting travel, and to a large extent in-person interactions, the pandemic has leveled the playing field in this particular instance. All of a sudden, it didn't matter where you were located. Whether you lived next door or on the other side of the world in India, it didn't matter. Interactions would still be remote over Zoom, and you would still have the same experience. The only real difference was time zones. Depending on where you lived, you may need to get up in the middle of the night to join a Zoom call, which by itself is a far smaller barrier than the need to travel thousands of miles away, and a barrier that any dedicated entrepreneur would be happy to overcome.

I was surprised to see the geographical diversity within our batch. I expected the vast majority of participants to be American, with a few Canadians like myself, and a small handful of internationals. But I was wrong. Looking at where my batchmates were located, in addition to cities in North America, I was surprised to see Bogota, Mexico City, Belo Horizonte, Hyderabad, Newcastle, Chandigarh, Buenos Aires, Padua, Providencia, Jakarta, and Cairo. While YC has been open to international participation for some time, my anecdotal observations led me to believe that this was not the same as past years; there were more internationals than before.

As I got to know my fellow entrepreneurs in my batch, I soon realized that no small number of them were able to participate in this batch purely because it was remote. Take Greg for example, an entrepreneur I had the pleasure of getting to know through a remote meeting arranged by Donut. Living in North Carolina, married with a wife and two teenage kids, the prospect of moving 3,000 miles away to the other side of the country, separated by three time zones, for three months, was too much of a sacrifice to fathom. And this sacrifice would not only be for him. His two co-founders, who also had children, would need to make the same decision. For all of them and their families, moving to San Francisco for YC was a tough sell, and they would have said no if it had not been remote. This conversation triggered another profound realization about the pandemic's effect on the relationship between age and entrepreneurship.

If you're a common reader of tech entrepreneurship opinion pieces, it would be of no surprise to you to occasionally come across an article lamenting the ageism that exists in entrepreneurship. Entrepreneurship is often associated with the young, those in their twenties and thirties. In today's day and age, when you think of entrepreneurs, you conjure up images of Mark Zuckerberg with Facebook, Bill Gates with Microsoft, Steve Jobs with Apple, and Larry Page with Google. All of these titans built their companies and rose to prominence as young people in their twenties and thirties.

In addition, the entrepreneurial journey often requires a high degree of flexibility and adaptability. You may need to move countries or cities, you may need to work long and unconventional hours, and you may need to be available at a moment's call. So the fewer commitments you have in life, obviously the easier it is for you to be flexible and adaptable. It's much easier to move to another country or work unconventional hours when you have few or no family commitments.

Of course, the older you get, the more likely that you're going to have a family, and the more likely it is that you also have children. These familial commitments can often be a barrier to participating in start-up programs, as my conversation with Greg helped me realize. When one has to choose between participating in a start-up program and living at home with the family, it's not surprising that most people would choose family.

But what if you could do both? And with our new remote world, that is now a possibility. As I sat in front of my computer speaking over Zoom with Greg in North Carolina, it dawned on me that this pandemic, in a unique way, is opening up the world instead of isolating it. It has indirectly enabled people like Greg, who don't fit the conventional image of a young, ambitious entrepreneur, to access programs that in the past he would not have been able to.

As my mind continued to churn and ponder on what dimensions other than age and geography has the pandemic opened, I was curious to investigate the size of our batch relative to those who had come before. Digging into the records, I observed that our current batch was in fact the largest batch ever to be accepted by YC: over two hundred companies. Compared to the last batch just six months ago, it was an increase of almost 20 percent.

Thinking as to why that could be case, it suddenly clicked in my mind. Space was no longer a limiting factor. In this new world that the pandemic has created, physical spaces are no longer necessary to hold events. This is profound, as it means the only limits to event size participation is the ability to maintain the quality of the program as the number of participants grow.

At the start of the pandemic, I foresaw the effects of the pandemic on my entrepreneurial journey as curses and challenges. But as the weeks and months went by, and my mind was opened through conversation and new experiences, I began to count the pandemic's effects not as curses but rather as blessings.

If the pandemic did not put a restriction on travel, my partner and I would have eagerly moved down from Vancouver to San Francisco for three months. We would have found a tiny and absurdly priced apartment to rent, needed to furnish and make it homey, and spent a fortune getting over-priced takeout in one of the most expensive living regions in the world. I estimate it would have cost us at least $15,000.

We also would be distant from our business operations, which at the time were exclusively serving the metro Vancouver region. But most notably, we would have been away from our families. Knowing the personality of myself and my partner, this would most likely have led to a most unbalanced lifestyle.

With the two of us cooped up in a small apartment with no close friends and family nearby, we would have buried ourselves deep into our work. From morning til night, that is what we would talk about. This would create negative consequences in our family relationships, our physical health, and our mental health. No doubt, without balancing relationships with our wives, we would have worked ourselves to the bone and burnt out. But this did not happen, because instead of moving down, we had no choice but to stay put. And there is no doubt in my mind that our business and myself have come out better because of it.

My story is not unique. Thousands if not millions of entrepreneurs around the world are going through experiences that in some form or other echo mine. I know this to be true based on stories I've heard from people around the world through my participation with YC.

COVID has forced us all to change the way we do things by bringing a new semblance of reality upon us. And it has brought this change not only for three months, nor six months, but likely years. It has shaped entrepreneurship, society, and the entire world for decades to come.

With this new reality comes the opportunity to reshape the world in a positive way. From my front row vantage point, I have seen the opportunities to create a new world.

- A world where personal opportunities are not constrained by your geographical location and what is available locally, but instead constrained only by the power of your imagination and ambition.

- A world where people in differing stages of life and varying levels of familial commitments can pursue careers and dreams traditionally not available to them in a pre-pandemic world. Where people can make fewer tradeoffs between family versus work, settling down versus staying flexible.
- A more equitable world where those in developing countries or remote locations can access resources and programs that in the past they could not access.
- A world where housing is more affordable because where you choose to live is no longer dictated by where you choose to work.
- A world where meeting and connecting virtually with other humans is not only commonplace but as easy as the press of a single button on your phone.

As we move into the future we will be presented with the choice of whether we should revert back to the way we did things in a pre-COVID world. Realistically, we will not fully revert back to the way it was. Yes, some of us will return to working in our offices. Yes, we will gather in large groups to watch sports and attend concerts. But it will not be a 100 percent return back to the way it was. The effects of COVID will be long lasting, and in a sense it has imprinted itself onto our society and world permanently. As far as I can tell, a new world is being created.

While opportunities abound, we must not be naive in pretending that there are few challenges and hardships. For example, the increased dependency on technology sharpens the divide between those who have access to technology and those who do not. For those in developing countries who have access to a computer and an internet connection, this new world can become a more equitable one. But for their neighbor who does not have access to a computer or internet connection, a wedge is driven into their divide, and their world made less equitable. This challenge, and many more, await us in our post-pandemic world.

It is of vital importance for us to be aware of these challenges, for it is in these challenges that we can find unique opportunities to create a better, more equitable, and more accessible world. We cannot look at the pandemic as something impossible to overcome, nor as a burden that we only need to temporarily weather. Instead, we need to view it as a path to forge a new and brighter future for ourselves, for our children, and our children's children.

10

COVID, Color, Culture

Medicine's Hour of Reckoning

Allen H. Roberts II

An aging and rebound copy of Sir William Osler's *Principles and Practice of Medicine* resides inconspicuously in my living room barrister bookcase.[1] Originally published in 1892, Osler's iconic work was the standard text for medical education in this country for years; my maternal grandfather, a surgeon and medical missionary, imbibed its science and wisdom in the first years of the twentieth century, and my father, a general practitioner of the "old school," partook of an updated version in the decades that followed. "Principles and practice of medicine"—I love that grand phrase, as I have always loved medicine, and I think the title of the book is what has kept it on my shelf, a reminder of sorts that there is principle behind the practice.

1. William Osler, *The Principles and Practice of Medicine* (New York: D. Appleton, 1892).

There is no explicit delineation of *principle* from *practice* in this venerable text. What philosophic principles may guide the praxis of medicine are so conspicuously quiet that we might conclude that Osler did not recognize or embrace a philosophy of medicine. However, his extensive philosophical essays demonstrate that is far from the case. His pervasive concern was how physicians might habitually "live up to" the high call to the lofty profession of medicine.[2] What was it about the profession of medicine that made it a high calling? As we will see, it would fall to a future physician-ethicist to articulate more fully a philosophy of medicine, to state what medicine *is* and why it is such an honorable profession. But principle and practice remain useful categories as we think about COVID-19.

The then-contemporary lessons of medicine espoused in Osler' textbook, to be sure, were very much part of the professional mindset of the community of physicians, including my grandfather, who cared for the victims of the 1918 pandemic. The toll of that pandemic was inestimable, but the memory of it was, arguably, short-lived. Few of us who entered the medical profession by the 1970s gave a second thought to this historic and devastating disease, despite the living presence among us, not so many decades later, of so many who had suffered such great loss at its hands.

Did the 1918 event "change" the principles and practice of medicine? Will the current COVID-19 pandemic somehow change medicine? This is the question at hand. In this brief essay I suggest that the exigencies of containment, mitigation, and treatment of COVID-19 have already changed, and will continue to change, *how* we practice medicine. There is, after all, no disease or therapy

---

2. Examples may be found in his well-known essays, such as "Aequanimitas" and "The Master-Word in Medicine," in *The Collected Essays of William Osler, Vol. 1, The Philosophical Essays*, ed. John McGovern and Charles Roland (Birmingham: Classics of Medicine Library, 1985).

that ever leaves medicine unchanged in terms of scientific methodology and technique. But if medicine is indeed a high calling, then it remains so, and I contend that there is no disease that can fundamentally alter what the *profession of medicine is*. Therefore, rather than examining medicine through the lens of the pandemic, it will be a more worthy and fruitful endeavor to consider the pandemic from the perspective of medicine as a high calling.

Let us look at several dimensions of this disease that are of deep concern to all who practice and who lead our profession. My perspective is that of a practitioner of critical care medicine in a tertiary-care, university-based medical center who has taken care of critically ill patients with COVID-19 and who has shared a measure of hospital leadership responsibilities in addition to clinical duties during the COVID-19 crisis. My academic interests involve clinical bedside medical ethics, specifically the ethics that surround end-of-life care. In my opinion the clinical encounter of patient with physician is the heart of medicine, and the window into the larger enterprise of the profession, so this very encounter will figure significantly in the discussion.

In providing care to a patient who suffers from an acute illness which occurs in the setting of one or more chronic or "background" illnesses, the physician's task is to determine the contextualized impact of the acute, so-called "inter-current" illness without neglecting the implications of the patient's chronic diseases. Similarly, it will not do simply to dissect out what is transpiring in our profession today *solely* because of COVID-19 without attempting to understand this disease in the context of the long-festering but freshly acknowledged malignancy of racial disparities in healthcare delivery, or the acute toxicity of a divisive political season. More significantly, COVID-19 must be evaluated against the backdrop of certain societal norms which have been evolving over several decades, and which have called into question the historic moral agency and beneficence of our profession.

This admixture of medicine, COVID-19, racial disparity, cultural trends, and politics inevitably impacts the care that each patient receives, and the ethics of this convergence begins at the individual clinical encounter.

We begin with some definitions and a comment on the status of the pandemic in the US at the time of this writing. For simplicity we shall refer to the disease and pandemic as "COVID-19," and to the culprit virus as "coronavirus."[3] The pathophysiology and clinical manifestations of the disease have recently been reviewed.[4] Coronavirus is spread by way of respiratory droplets that are exhaled, spoken, laughed, or sung into aerosolized particles during close face-to-face contact;[5] patients may be asymptomatic, minimally symptomatic, or overtly and significantly symptomatic, and infectious to others at every stage. Face masks and social distancing are effective, unequivocally, in reducing the spread of coronavirus.[6] The average time from exposure to onset of clinical illness is five days, with 97 percent of patients developing symptoms within twelve days. Symptoms are predominantly those of acute lower respiratory tract infection, with fever, cough, and shortness of breath; some patients transiently lose a sense of taste

3. Whereas in common parlance we hear "COVID" in reference both to the virus and the pandemic, more accurate terminology refers to the coronavirus disease 2019 (COVID-19) pandemic, which is due to the novel severe acute respiratory syndrome coronavirus 2 (SARS-CoV-2).

4. W. Joost Wiersinga et al., "Pathophysiology, Transmission, Diagnosis, and Treatment of Coronavirus Disease 2019 (COVID-19)," *JAMA* 324, no. 8 (2020): 782–93.

5. L. Hamner et al., "High SARS-CoV-2 Attack Rate Following Exposure at a Choir Practice—Skagit County, Washington, March 2020," *MMWR Morb Mortal Wkly Rep* 69, May 15, 2020: 606.

6. Jeremy Howard et al., "An Evidence Review of Face Masks Against COVID-19," *Proceedings of the National Academy of Sciences of the United States of America* 118, no. 4, January 26, 2021.

and smell, and many have additional neurological manifestations. Disease can exist on the spectrum of mild to severe to fatal, with most deaths occurring because of respiratory failure caused by coronavirus pneumonia or by secondary pneumonia caused by bacteria (a phenomenon well known from the clinical course of influenza).

COVID-19 has affected millions. Death rates vary by patient age, with the highest rates seen in patients aged eighty-five or older. Up to 40 percent of patients who required intensive care unit admission died earlier in the pandemic.[7] Sepsis, multi-organ-system failure[8] and pulmonary embolism[9] contribute to mortality. And Hispanic and African American patients have borne, in this disease as in so many, the greater burden of illness and the higher toll of life.[10] Medical care is largely supportive, and balances state-of-the-art critical care with measures designed to minimize spread of the disease in the hospital. In so many illnesses, our supportive-care technology and methodology improves over time, and results in a lower mortality rate; the same has been seen in COVID-19.[11] A small number of pharmacologic agents, such as dexamethasone (a corticosteroid), remdesivir (an antiviral medication), and monoclonal antibodies have been found to reduce

7. Howard et al., "Evidence Review."

8. Howard et al., "Evidence Review."

9. Sigurd Lax et al., "Pulmonary Arterial Thrombosis in COVID-19 with Fatal Outcome," *Ann Int Med* 173, no. 5 (2000): 350–61.

10. Adia Wingfield, The Disproportionate Impact of COVID-19 on Black Health Care Workers in the US," available at https://hbr.org/2020/05/the-disproportionate-impact-of-COVID-19-on-black-health-care-workers-in-the-u-s, accessed September 10, 2020; and Merlin Chowkwanyum and Adolph Reed, Racial Health Disparities and COVID-19—Caution and Context," *NEJM* 383, no. 3 (2020): 201–3.

11. Leora Horwitz et al., "Trends in COVID-19 Risk-Adjusted Mortality Rates," *Journal of Hospital Medicine* 16, no. 2 (2021): 90–92.

the severity or duration of disease in some settings.[12] The available vaccinations against COVID-19 are highly effective in preventing severe disease and death.[13]

At the bedside clinical encounter, the devastation of this pandemic is neither "fake news" nor political conspiracy. Hundreds of thousands of patients in the United States have died from this disease. There are characteristic clinical signs, chest X-ray abnormalities, and death spirals. The commitment, self-sacrifice, and yes, the very *high calling* of the medical profession has never been more apparent than during the seemingly interminable COVID-19 crisis.

Studies of survivors of critical illness due to non-COVID-19 coronavirus diseases (MERS and SARS), as well as of other clinical entities such as sepsis, disclose a significant incidence of post-traumatic stress disorder, depression, anxiety, respiratory impairment and poor quality of life.[14] It is likely that these findings will be mirrored in COVID-19 survivors. However, we cannot know with certainty the full impact of the disease on the overall and organ-specific health of a COVID survivor. Similarly, whereas medical, regulatory, and lay literature brims with reports of the various aspects of healthcare delivery that have been acutely impacted by COVID-19, it would be premature to predict the long-term impact of the pandemic on certain practical and process-oriented aspects of medicine.

There are two process-related dimensions of the COVID-19 pandemic that bear mention as they relate to our thesis. One has to

12. For a concise and update summary, please refer to https://www.COVID19 treatmentguidelines.nih.gov/.

13. Heidi Moline et al., Effectiveness of COVID-19 Vaccines in Preventing Hospitalization Among Adults Age > 65 Years—COVID NET, 13 States, February–April 2021," *MMWR* 70, no. 32 (2021): 1088–93.

14. Hallie Prescott and Timothy Gerard, "Recovery from Severe COVID-19: Leveraging the Lessons of Survival from Sepsis," *JAMA* 324, no. 8 (2020): 739–40.

do with the nature of the clinical encounter during COVID-19, the other with decision making for the most critically ill.

Long before the pandemic, the use of telemedicine had been on the rise, both in primary care and in multiple specialties, not least in general medicine, neurology, and psychiatry. Even intensive care may be delivered "remotely" by physicians in medical centers who are overseeing the care of critically ill patients in more rural hospital venues. As a matter of resource utilization, efficiency of care and cost containment, electronic consultation with specialists is firmly established and growing.[15] Maintaining some measure of in-person clinical practice during widespread closures, on the one hand, while managing disease containment, on the other, was made possible by this very technological asset. It seems that there are a number of advantages to telemedicine that may endure into the pandemic's aftermath.[16] There is no question that many visits require the actual presence of patient with physician, but as medicine during the pandemic is demonstrating, telemedicine may actually liberate time in the physician's clinic schedule for those in-person visits that are more critical in terms of diagnostics and therapeutics.

John Barry, in his award-winning account of the 1918 influenza pandemic, rightly noted that the advent of stethoscope and laryngoscope in the nineteenth century signaled the first small physical separation of physician from patient, but that was part and parcel of medical progress.[17] Telemedicine is of the same cloth. Each instrument borne of new patient-care technologies will im-

15. Salman Ahmed et al., "Utility, Appropriateness, and Content of Electronic Consultations Across Medical Subspecialties: A Cohort Study," *Ann Int Med* 172, no. 10 (2020): 641–47.

16. Rachel Werner and Sherry Glied, "COVID-induced Changes in Health Care Delivery—Can They Last? *NEJM* 385, no. 10 (2021): 868–70.

17. John M. Barry, *The Great Influenza: The Story of the Deadliest Pandemic in History* (New York: Penguin, 2018), 26.

pose, as a byproduct of medical benefit, a measure of distance between patient and physician, but these same technologies actually preserve the *clinical encounter* and have the potential to augment, rather than diminish, the whole of the service that can be provided by physician to patient.

The second process-related issue in COVID-19 represents the latest expression of an abiding ethical dilemma that goes to the heart of the profession's nature. As hospitals, healthcare systems, and local and state governments prepared for a surge in patient numbers that had the potential to outstrip available assets, such as ICU beds and mechanical ventilators, a number of recommendations were published regarding the most appropriate way to allocate or reallocate limited resources. In contemporary, non-resource-constrained medical practice, patients receive care on a first-come, first-served basis; any critically ill patient who wishes to have life-sustaining measures in the ICU, such as intubation and mechanical ventilation, dialysis, or hemodynamic support with "pressor" medication, may be admitted to the ICU, and such measures may be instituted and continued. Patients or their surrogate decision makers may similarly decline such interventions, many times by advance directive. If high-tech life sustaining measures have been started, patients may also, by advance directive or surrogate decision, have life support discontinued if, in the opinion of the medical team, these interventions are deemed to be futile—that is, they no longer serve as a bridge to a prior state of health or to a definitive treatment but rather only prolong and complicate the inevitable dying process.

These end-of-life decisions are difficult under the best of circumstances. Once a cure or restoration of health is deemed not to be a realistic prospect, the decision to "withdraw" is more emotionally fraught than a decision to "forego" might have been. But these decisions can be ethical and legal when supported by the patient's own clinical prognosis, by evidence-based, statistical prognostic tools,[18] and by a process of shared decision-making by the family and a beneficent healthcare team—all within the contexts of moral law, community, and a paradigm of absolute human worth and dignity. These several dimensions—clinical prognostic data, shared decision making, and moral context—are indispensable for end-of-life decisions to be ethical and legal. If any of these is missing, the ethical and legal legitimacy of these decisions may be compromised.

The pandemic serves as exemplar for any crisis in which the demand for assets, such as ICU beds and ventilators, exceeds their supply. In the early months of COVID-19, many jurisdictions across the US, anticipating a massive surge of patients needing ICU-level of care, responded by expanding numbers of ICU beds in hospitals, and by opening public spaces such as the Javits Center in New York and the Washington Convention Center in DC as "field hospitals." But they also established utilitarian-based protocols for allocating limited resources if the demand remained unmet; these are generally referred to as plans for "modified delivery of care in crisis situations," or *crisis standards* of care. Such standards are thoughtful and evidence-based—up to a point. Crisis standards do endorse clinical data metrics (individual patient data, for instance, that indicate non-survivability) in decision making, and do so via physiologic scoring systems[19] that have been validated and are useful in some settings, but which have never been validated in mass-casualty situations; indeed, it is difficult to imagine how

18. Such as, when appropriate, physiologic scoring systems. Please see A. Rapsang and D. Shyam, "Scoring Systems in the Intensive Care Unit: A Compendium," *Indian J Crit Care Med* 18, no. 4 (2014): 220–28, for a concise review of currently used systems.

19. A comprehensive review of crisis standards may be found in Emily Machanda et al., "Crisis Standards of Care in the USA: A Systematic Review," *Journal of Racial and Ethnic Health Disparities* (2020); this paper does not endorse a specific set of criteria. https://www.ncbi.nlm.nih.gov/pmc/articles/PMC7425256/.

such validation could ever be accomplished. Additionally, some versions of these protocols provide for the codified application of *age, mental health* and *most-life-years-saved* criteria to the algorithm of who will be denied—or involuntarily removed from—mechanical ventilation if the ventilator is needed by someone who is younger, or whose "life-year-potential" has not been realized "as fully" as the patient who is otherwise next in line or who is already on the ventilator. Programs assigning such a "relativized worthiness" to older/more-life-years-lived patients have been proposed by Charles Sprung[20] and endorsed by Douglas White[21] and Ezekiel Emanuel.[22]

A number of protocols have suggested an allocation priority status for physicians and other health-care professionals who are COVID-stricken, citing the critical need of these individuals for the greater good;[23] other scholars have eschewed such special "professional courtesy" considerations as arbitrary.[24] It is not clear whether or to what extent such considerations have made it into mainline modified-standards algorithms.

Disability rights advocates have raised concerns about subjectively and externally applied "quality of life" bias in allocation algorithms; Hastings Center, University of Colorado and

20. Charles Sprung et al., "Adult ICU Triage During the Coronavirus Disease 2019 Pandemic: Who Will Live and Who Will Die? Recommendations to Improve Survival," *Critical Care Medicine* 48, no. 8 (2020): 1196–1202. The paper contains a "typical" triage algorithm that is quite informative.

21. Douglas White, "A Framework for Rationing Ventilators and Critical Care Beds During the COVID-19 Pandemic," *JAMA* 323, no. 18 (2020): 1773–74.

22. Ezekiel Emanuel et al., "Fair Allocation of Scarce Medical Resources in the Time of COVID 19," *NEJM* (2020).

23. Sprung et al., "Adult ICU Triage."

24. Lee Biddison et al., "Ethical Considerations—Care of the Critically Ill and Injured During Pandemics and Disasters: CHEST Consensus Statement," *Chest* 146, no. 4 supp. (2014): e145S–e155S.

Georgetown ethicists have endorsed these concerns, advocating that an "equal moral worth of all people," rather than subjective criteria, be used in triage and allocation programs.[25] The Christian Medical and Dental Associations (CMDA) Ethics Committee has challenged the age and life-years-saved criteria as being non-evidence-based, externally imposed and hidden forms of social valuation which place the vulnerable aged at risk. The CMDA holds that all lives are of inestimable value regardless of years lived,[26] and that the criteria of age and life-years saved should not enter triage equations. And in the United States, the federal government successfully obtained revision of protocols by multiple providers and public health entities, which would have permitted allocating medical care on the basis of quality-of-life or years-of-life considerations, on the grounds that those protocols would have violated statutory and constitutional protections against discrimination on the basis of age and disability.[27] Thus the "acute illness" of the COVID-19 pandemic.

25. Mildred Solomon et al., "COVID-19 Crisis Triage—Optimizing Outcomes and Disability Rights," *NEJM* (2020).

26. Paul Hoehner et al, Triage and Resource Allocation During Crisis Medical Surge Conditions (Pandemics and Mass Casualty Situations): A Position Paper of the Christian Medical and Dental Associations Special Task Force," *Christian Journal of Global Health* 7, no. 1 (2020).

27. In March 2020, as responses to the pandemic were just gearing up nationwide and such protocols were coming to light, Roger Severino, Director of the US Department of Health & Human Services Office for Civil Rights, announced settlements with multiple providers over protocols that could have violated Section 504 of the Rehabilitation Act of 1973, Title II of the Americans with Disabilities Act, Section 1557 of the Patient Protection and Affordable Care Act, and the Age Discrimination Act of 1975: "Decisions by covered entities concerning whether an individual is a candidate for treatment should be based on an individualized assessment of the patient based on the best available objective medical evidence. . . . Persons with disabilities should not be denied medical care on the basis of

We turn now to attend to the first of the "chronic conditions," which must also be considered where our response to COVID is concerned. Three decades ago, the Council on Ethical and Judicial Affairs (CEJA) of the American Medical Association (AMA) published a landmark paper describing long-standing and marked disparities in health care afforded to African American patients across a number of specialties in the US, reporting that these disparities have their roots in socioeconomic factors, educational disparities, and failures by the medical profession. The authors proposed several broad-stroked recommendations for the amelioration of these disparities.[28] The value of this paper today, lamentably, is its historical testimony that so little has actually been accomplished by society or by the profession over these intervening thirty years to take seriously the disparities or to mitigate them meaningfully. Additional research has disclosed that both intentional and unintentional racial biases in medicine are deeply imbedded psychologically.[29] Quite apart from COVID-19, even palliative and hospice end-of-life services are unequally available to minorities.[30]

At the height of the pandemic in May 2020, the death of George Floyd coincided with the evolving epidemiological aware-

---

stereotypes, assessments of quality of life, or judgments about a person's relative "worth" based on the presence or absence of disabilities or age." "Our Civil Rights Laws Protect the Equal Dignity of Every Human Life from Ruthless Utilitarianism," https://www.hhs.gov/sites/default/files/ocr-bulletin-3–28–20.pdf.

28. Council on Ethical and Judicial Affairs, "Black-white Disparities in Health Care," *JAMA* 263, no. 17 (1990): 2344–46.

29. John Dovidio et al., Disparities and Distrust: The Implications of Psychological Processes for Understanding Racial Disparities in Health and Health Care," *Social Science & Medicine* (2008).

30. Katherine Ornstein et al, Evaluation of Racial Disparities in Hospice and End-of-Life Treatment Intensity in the REGARDS Cohort," *JAMA Network Open* 3, no. 8 (2020).

ness that people of color were suffering disproportionately from COVID-19, and that death rates in blacks and Hispanics were higher than in whites. This sad confluence of tragedies has resulted in what many have called a "time of reckoning" in the United States for the all-pervasive and deeply rooted societal discrimination against people of color, and this reckoning rightly has come to the doorstep of the profession of medicine itself. Chowkwanyum and Reed have written a thoughtful and balanced account of the origins and practical impact of racial disparities in the setting of COVID-19, addressing the root causes of inequity in both clinical and research methodology. These causes include erroneous assumptions of biological differences between racial groups, racial stereotyping of behavioral patterns, and geographical stigmatization.[31] A large volume of literature is now being produced on the matter, with what seems to be fresh energy to address these disparities in ways that are sound of scholarship and method.

The second "chronic condition" against which COVID-19 must be seen is that of the significant shift of ethical norms that has occurred in medicine over the past several decades. Most of us who practice clinical medicine have been raised on the so-called "Georgetown Mantra,"[32] that is, the ethical principles of patient autonomy, physician beneficence and non-maleficence, and justice. Most ethical considerations at the bedside or in the consultation

31. Merlin Chowkwanyum and Adolph Reed, Racial Health Disparities and COVID-19—Caution and Context," *NEJM* 383, no. 3 (2020): 201–3.

32. See, for example, S. M. Gallagher, "The Ethics of Compassion," *Ostomy Wound Management* 45, no. 6 (1999): 14–16. The term likely derives from the contribution of Tom Beauchamp of Georgetown University, to the study of biomedical ethics (see n25). "The Georgetown Mantra of Bioethics, which includes the principles of beneficence, non-maleficence, autonomy, and justice, has largely been regarded as the mainstay of ethical principles in the healthcare setting. Moral or ethical decisions have been discussed using this framework." Available at https://pubmed.ncbi.nlm.nih.gov/10655857/, accessed October 15, 2020.

room turn on the relative weight and contribution of each of these principles in a given situation; a comprehensive review and functional treatment of medical principlism may be found in the work of Beauchamp and Childress, *Principles of Biomedical Ethics*, now in its eighth edition.[33] In practice and in ethics consultation, these principles are generally held in balance, usually with the patient's *autonomy* being in balance with the physician's *beneficence* and *non-maleficence*. There was a time in medicine in the US when a physician's beneficence assumed the phenotype of paternalism, but that has largely and happily changed as physicians' beneficence has learned to walk in step with patients' autonomy.

Recent decades, however, have seen the ascent of patient autonomy to be the primary driving principle in all medical ethical decisions, driven by an anthropology that Robert Bellah refers to as "expressive individualism";[34] beneficence, non-maleficence and justice, effectively have been subordinated.[35] This phenomenon is witnessed most dramatically in the public debate over physician-assisted suicide (PAS),[36] also known as medical-aid-in-dying (MAID).[37] The ancient and abiding moral *proscription* of phy-

---

33. Tom L. Beauchamp and James F. Childress, *Principles of Biomedical Ethics* (Oxford: Oxford University Press, 2019).

34. Robert Bellah et al, *Habits of the Heart: Individualism and Commitment in American Life* (Berkeley: University of California Press, 1985), 334.

35. Madison Kilbride and Steven Joffe, "The New Age of Patient Autonomy," *JAMA* 320, no. 19 (2018): 1973–74.

36. A comprehensive review of the intersection of expressive individualism and end-of-life choices may be found in O. Carter Snead, *What It Means to Be Human: The Case for the Body in Public Bioethics* (Cambridge, MA: Harvard University Press, 2020), 256.

37. Scholarly ethical parlance includes such terms as voluntary and involuntary, active and passive euthanasia. In common parlance, broadly speaking, the general term "physician-assisted suicide" refers to the practice of a patient who is terminally ill requesting and receiving from his or her physician a prescription

sicians' intentionally ending their patients' lives, has, in the past twenty years, been discarded by a number of states and the District of Columbia. Certain patients' rights advocacy groups have targeted legislatures across the country with a campaign for legalization of PAS, buoyed by widespread media coverage of the tragic case of Brittany Maynard, who suffered from brain cancer and who ended her life through PAS in 2014. Increasing numbers of physicians and of the public are embracing the practice as legitimate.[38] (It is important to recall, at this juncture, that African Americans, with their long-standing, disparity-driven distrust of medicine, historically have been opposed to PAS.)[39]

There is scholarly legal sentiment that PAS will pave the way for active euthanasia in the US,[40] despite the reaffirmation of the decades-old proscription of this practice by both the American

---

for a lethal medication, the self-ingestion of which (by mouth) results in the intentional ending of the patient's life. "Active euthanasia," on the other hand, refers to the patient requesting, and the physician or nurse actively administering, a lethal drug intravenously.

38. Ezekiel Emanuel et al., "Attitudes and Practices of Euthanasia and Physician-Assisted Suicide in the United States, Canada, and Europe," *JAMA* 316, no. 1 (2016): 79–90.

39. Richard Lichtenstein et al., Black/White Differences in Attitudes Toward Physician-Assisted Suicide," *Journal of the National Medical Association* 89, no. 2 (1997): 125–33. See also http://patientsrightscouncil.org/site/inequities-for-minorities-and-poor/ and Terri Laws, "How Race Matters in the Physician-Assisted Suicide Debate," in *Religion and Politics*, https://religionandpolitics.org/print/?pid=15682.

40. John Keown, *Euthanasia, Ethics and Public Policy*, 2nd ed. (Cambridge: Cambridge University Press, 2018), 458.

College of Physicians[41] in 2017 and the AMA[42] in 2019. Sulmasy has pointed out that the same moral arguments that are made in defense of PAS may be justifiably made for euthanasia.[43] The premise of legitimizing PAS, to be sure, is that a person's only real dignity is realized in her ability to have her wishes granted;[44] physicians, on this argument, are to act as technicians whose moral agency is non-existent or irrelevant. Opponents of the practice of PAS have argued that it violates the moral order, being indifferent to the community at large,[45] particularly the vulnerable elderly, who may be at risk of being coerced under real or perceived financial, social, or emotional pressures.[46]

Just as we have seen the intersection of COVID-19 and longstanding racial healthcare disparity, here also we see the inevitable intersection of the pandemic with the practices of assisted death. Already there have been reports of COVID-19-related increases in suicidal ideation in at-risk populations,[47] and that an increased risk of suicide among COVID-19 survivors is likely to persist into

41. Lois Snyder Sulmasy and Paul Mueller, Ethics and the Legalization of Physician-Assisted Suicide: An American College of Physicians Position Paper," *Ann Int Med* 167, no. 8 (2017): 576–78.

42. https://www.ama-assn.org/delivering-care/ethics/physician-assisted-suicide.

43. Daniel Sulmasy et al, "Response to Ezekiel et al (2016)," *JAMA* 316, no. 15 (2016): 1600.

44. Ruth Macklin, "Dignity Is a Useless Concept," *British Medical Journal* 327 (2003): 1419–20.

45. Allen Roberts, "Response to Sulmasy and Mueller (letter)," *Ann Int Med* 168, no. 11 (2018): 834.

46. Allen Roberts, "Physician-assisted Suicide: A Christian Response," *Modern Reformation* 27, no. 2 (2018): 9–12.

47. Mark Cziesler et al, "Mental Health, Substance Abuse, and Suicidal Ideation During the COVID-19 Pandemic," *MMWR* 69, no. 32 (2020): 1049–57.

the aftermath of the pandemic.[48] In the setting of crisis-standards of healthcare delivery, for patients who, by arbitrary and subjective criteria may be removed involuntarily from a ventilator on a utilitarian model of resource allocation, the door is open for them to request, and receive, assistance in dying.[49] Ample precedent for such a tendency has been described in the Canadian experience with PAS and euthanasia.[50]

In summary, the horrid COVID-19 pandemic, in the sweep of history, cannot be dissected out and appraised in isolation, but only and inescapably within the context of deep racial disparities that have persisted for centuries, and of a societal shift away from moral norms that have prevailed for millennia. So much good has been done by so many health care providers for so many afflicted patients and families in these endless months. Yet behind the scenes lurk dark ethical problems, which, one might surmise, are themselves symptomatic of a deeper systemic malady.

COVID-19 has served to highlight the most promising but also the most troubling aspects of our medical culture and profession. In this latter category, the common denominator is the systematized, programmatic, and *prescriptive* tendency, in all cases, toward a *relativizing of human worth*. All human history bears lamentable witness to this tendency, now manifest again amid COVID-19 in racial bias; in arbitrary, state-sponsored, utilitarian guidance for scarce resource allocation; and in the minds of the burdened dying that their lives are, finally, of less or no value.

48. Leo Sher, "The Impact of the COVID-19 Pandemic on Suicide Rates," *QJM: An International Journal of Medicine* 113, no. 10 (2020): 707–12.

49. Jeffrey Berger, "Pandemic Preparedness Planning: Will Provisions for Involuntary Termination of Life Support Invite Active Euthanasia?," *The Journal of Clinical Ethics* 21, no. 4 (2010): 308–11.

50. Brian Bird, "Expanding Euthanasia During the Pandemic," *The Public Discourse*, available at https://www.thepublicdiscourse.com/2020/06/64288/.

How then, might COVID-19 bring about a change in medicine? Our hand, as a profession, is being called. Have we lost sight of a binding philosophic North Star in medicine? Does one even exist? I will suggest that COVID-19, within its unavoidable contexts of culture and color, provides the very occasion for *reflection, repentance, and reformation* within the profession. I draw from religious norms, but their call is relevant to persons of good will of all faiths and no faith.

In his study of the Protestant Reformation, scientist and theologian Alister McGrath writes that the Reformers, employing the philosophic methodology of the humanism of the Renaissance, sought to return *ad fontes*, that is, "to the sources," or original documents of the faith, in their original languages.[51] As we avail ourselves of the COVID-19 experience to look afresh at the nature of the medical profession, specifically with an eye to some task of reformation, it will be useful similarly to look carefully to the sources of our profession from its earliest philosophic iteration.

Naturally we turn to Hippocrates and the tradition that bears his name, as a primitive yet enduring articulation of the nature of medicine. The tenets of the Hippocratic Oath, and of the corpus of medical writing ascribed to the Hippocratic tradition, are informative both in terms of the virtue incumbent upon physicians and of the honored status in which they were to hold both their patients and their profession. The Oath itself forbids assisted suicide, abortion, the breaching of confidence, and the sexual exploitation of patients, male or female, slave or free—thus protecting, through the moral agency of the virtuous physician, the most vulnerable and marginalized of society. Explicit in the oath is a code of vir-

---

51. Alister McGrath, *Reformation Thought: An Introduction* (Malden, MA: Blackwell, 1999), 41–45. McGrath indicates that whereas the term "humanism" was not used in Renaissance literature, it has its roots in the sixteenth century describing a "literary scholar," that is, one versed in ancient tongues.

tuous conduct to which physicians must adhere; implicit is the recognition of the *worthiness* of their patients of such protection. Nothing like this had ever been seen in the ancient world. Physicians and medicine were held to a standard of virtue, and *all* patients were regarded to be sacred. In his day, Hippocrates was countercultural.[52]

To be sure, Hippocrates and his oath have serious and worthy critics today, including Robert Veatch, who has questioned the "paternalistic" premises and therefore the legitimacy of the tradition,[53] and who has, on these grounds, pronounced the Hippocratic ethic to be dead.[54] Even those who are sympathetic to Hippocrates acknowledge the diluted influence of the oath in medical schools over the course of the twentieth century.[55] Many today would blithely relegate the Hippocratic narrative to the relic heap of history.

But the Hippocratic tradition was an early iteration of the virtues of antiquity taking the form of virtue ethics, which became woven into—and *redefined*—the profession of medicine. Both Hippocratic tradition and the Oath were constructs of ancient Greek thought and Pythagorean philosophy; physicians were "accountable" to pagan deities. The fact that there was accountability to the "divine" lent itself to the adaptation of the tenets of the tradition by

---

52. Nigel Cameron, *The New Medicine: Life and Death After Hippocrates* (Chicago: Bioethics Press, 1991). Cameron provides a comprehensive history of the context of the Hippocratic Oath and tradition.

53. Robert Veatch, "Hippocratic, Religious, and Secular Ethics: The Points of Conflict," *Theoretical Medicine and Bioethics* 33, no. 1 (2012): 33–43.

54. Robert Veatch, "The Hippocratic Ethic Is Dead," *The New Physician*, September 1984, 41–48.

55. Robert Orr et al., "Use of the Hippocratic Oath: A Review of Twentieth Century Practice and Content Analysis of Oaths Administered in Medical Schools in the US and Canada in 1993," *J Clin Ethics* 8, no. 4 (1997): 377–88.

the Abrahamic religions;[56] quietly, the Oath and tradition affirmed patients to be *sacred* and their interests worthy of protection, and this affirmation governed medicine for over two millennia.

What Hippocrates saw, if through a glass darkly, his Judeo-Christian interpreters understood more fully to be the defining principle of all ethics, namely that each person is created in *imago Dei*—in God's image[57]—and at least on the Christian understanding, that tending to the sick carries unspeakable eschatological significance.[58] David Gushee sums it up:

> Human life is sacred: this means that God has consecrated each and every human being—without exception and in all circumstances—as a unique, incalculably precious being of elevated status and dignity. Through God's revelation in Scripture and incarnation in Jesus Christ, God has declared and demonstrated the sacred worth of human beings and will hold us accountable for responding appropriately. Such a response...includes offering due respect and care to each human being that we encounter.[59]

The erosion of the Hippocratic and Abrahamic religious influences in recent generations, not least in a post-modern age that eyes all metanarrative askance, lends urgency to the reacquisition of a virtue-based ethics in medicine. One does not need to adhere to an Abrahamic faith to acknowledge and claim the benefit of an absolute sacredness model; such a model lends the utmost protection to the most vulnerable, and arguably provides the final and only cogent rationale for such protection.

56. Cameron, *New Medicine*, 41.

57. Genesis 1:27.

58. Matthew 25:31–46.

59. David Gushee, *The Sacredness of Human Life: Why an Ancient World Biblical Vision Is Key to the World's Future* (Grand Rapids: Eerdmans, 2013), 411.

Chief among advocates for just such a renewed absolute-sacredness/virtue-ethics paradigm is the late Dr. Edmund Pellegrino (1920–2013),[60] who, writing from a decidedly Aristotelian-Thomistic standpoint, set forth a philosophy of medicine that may be claimed by the secular as well as the religious of all traditions. Pellegrino argued for a reclamation of medicine which recasts the Hippocratic *worthiness of the patient* in the balanced context of beneficence with autonomy. His contributions include a critical re-evaluation of Hippocrates in light of contemporary concerns (effectively answering Veatch's charges),[61] and he was among the first to embark on the exploration of African American medical ethics.[62]

Pellegrino taught that whereas principlism and rule-based ethical formulae have been ascendant in recent decades, the physi-

60. A native of Newark, Dr. Pellegrino was raised and educated in New York City with Catholic roots. He attended Xavier High School, St. John's University, Queens, and New York University. A Christian physician, philosopher, bioethicist, and academic, he published 605 articles and chapters and twenty-four books on medical science, philosophy, and medical ethics, remaining active in all disciplines into the final months of his life (he died at 93 in 2013). Over his professional career he held positions as President of the Catholic University of America; at Georgetown he was Director of the Kennedy Institute of Ethics, John Carroll Professor of Medicine and Medical Ethics, founder of the Center for Clinical Bioethics (now the Pellegrino Center), and founder of the Center for the Advanced Study of Ethics. He was a Master of the American College of Physicians, Fellow of the Hastings Center, Chair of the President's Council on Bioethics, and Senior Fellow of the Center for Bioethics and Human Dignity. Pellegrino has been referred to as "the father of modern medical ethics."

61. Edmund Pellegrino, "Toward an Expanded Medical Ethics: The Hippocratic Ethic Revisited," in *The Philosophy of Medicine Reborn: A Pellegrino Reader* (Notre Dame: Notre Dame University Press, 2008), 401.

62. See Lawrence Prograis and Edmund Pellegrino, *African American Bioethics: Culture Race, and Identity* (Washington, DC: Georgetown University Press, 2004).

cian's *virtue* "remains an inescapable reality in moral transactions .
. . their moral effectiveness still turns on the disposition and character traits of our fellow men and women. . . . This is preeminently true in medical ethics, where the vulnerability and dependence of the sick person force him or her to trust not just in her rights, but in the kind of person the physician is."[63] The physician must be virtuous—for the good of the patient. Virtues incumbent on the physician are fidelity to the patient's trust, benevolence, self-sacrifice, compassion, intellectual integrity and honesty, justice, empathy, and prudence.[64] Now more than ever, there is a need for the virtues *to be woven into and to redefine medicine.* Where does this start?

In general, virtue ethics in medicine presupposes that the *telos* of medicine is the *good of the patient.* Our individual virtues, our character as physicians, are to be directed to the good of the patient. The question is, what constitutes the "good of the patient?" Pellegrino places the cornerstone of the patient's good in the one-on-one personal encounter of patient with physician, familiar and dear to all of us, which is

> the activity that defines physicians qua physicians, and sets them apart from other persons who may have medical knowledge but do not use it specifically in clinical encounters with individual patients. Clinical medicine is the *locus ethicus* whose end is a right and good healing action and decision. Moreover, clinical medicine is the final pathway through which public policies ultimately come to affect the lives of sick persons. Finally, no matter how broad or socially oriented we may make medicine, illness remains a human experience, and its impact on individual human persons remains why medicine and physicians exist in the first place.[65]

---

63. E. Pellegrino and D. Thomasma, *For the Patient's Good: The Restoration of Beneficence in Health Care* (Oxford: Oxford University Press, 1988), 112.

64. Pellegrino, "Toward an Expanded Medical Ethics," 272.

65. Pellegrino, "Toward an Expanded Medical Ethics," 66.

The "right and good healing action," which is the fruit of the patient encounter, is, finally, the end of medicine.

Pellegrino contends that "medicine exists because being ill and being healed are universal human experiences, not because society has created medicine as a practice. Rather than a social construct, the nature of medicine, its internal goods and virtues, are defined by the ends of medicine, and therefore, ontologically internal from the outset."[66] There are four dimensions of the "patient's good" in this concept, which include the biomedical good, which results from correct application of skilled and judiciously chosen interventions, the patient's perception of his own good in any given clinical situation, the good of humans generally (that is, the community), and the spiritual good of the patient.[67]

All four "goods" are necessarily bounded by the moral order and are guarded by what has been described as an "internal morality" of medicine. Medicine, insists Pellegrino, is possessed of an intrinsic morality that is not defined or validated by physicians or by the profession; the authority of this internal morality is independent of whether physicians accept it. "[This] authority," he writes, "arises from an objective order of morality that transcends the self-defined goals of a profession."[68] The *telos* of medicine, and hence its internal morality, are not subject to constraints of time, religion, social programs, nor to the preferences or whims of an autonomous individual. To summarize, virtue ethics is derived from the natural, or moral, law that is acknowledgeable by all. In this ethics paradigm, the virtue of the individual moral agent is the centerpiece of ethical behavior and action.

Just as Hippocrates was countercultural in his day, so too, necessarily, will be a reformation of medicine in our own. That

---

66. Pellegrino, "Toward an Expanded Medical Ethics," 66.
67. Pellegrino, "Toward an Expanded Medical Ethics," 72–75.
68. Pellegrino, "Toward an Expanded Medical Ethics," 68.

considerable public opinion—asserting incontestable personal autonomy as the phenotype of expressive individualism—favors the legalization of physician-assisted death means that a renewed Hippocratic "absolute sacredness" paradigm will face a difficult upstream swim. But if medicine is to remain what medicine is—a high calling, possessed of its own ontological beneficence and internal morality—then so be it.

The lesson of the COVID-19 pandemic—against the backdrop of historic racial injustice and of societal jettisoning of normative morality—is to recover to our mindset and worldview the absolute and abiding sacredness of every human life, undiminished by age or affliction, and the imminent eschatological mandate to provide care equitably across all lines and at all stages of life, especially life's end. This is the only possible starting point of a medical reformation.

We in the profession of medicine must deeply reflect. It is one thing to assert the virtues of the physician and the beneficence and internal morality of the profession itself against the intrusion of utilitarian ethics in medical triage and of a decontextualized and inflated "autonomy" model in end-of-life choices. It is quite another to come to terms with the fact of our own complicity in the creation and sustenance of deep racial and socioeconomic disparities that do, finally, come home to violate our very clinical encounters, which are so deeply cherished. And members of our own profession have become champions of the assisted death agenda. We are well advised to attend to the lethal log of racial disparity that is in the eye of our own profession, so that we might see more clearly to remove the fatal speck from the eye of those who would cross the lines to endorse and practice assisted death. Medicine must attend to this latter crime as well, without neglecting the more subtly institutionalized fractures of the moral law.

A time of individual and professional repentance and rededication to a virtue ethic that acknowledges the absolute sacredness of every human life is at hand for medicine. The *principle* of absolute sacredness is, finally, behind Osler's and our own *practice*. It is not that medicine must redefine itself; medicine is ontologically defined, as Pellegrino has insisted. And this will not be medicine's first reformation, as Barry has reminded us in his account of the history leading up to the 1918 pandemic.[69] If the reformation in US medicine in the late nineteenth century was necessarily *scientific* in nature, the current one must be *ethical* in nature.

COVID-19, like all diseases before it, will certainly change the practical dimensions of medicine. But the profession of medicine, the skilled, scholarly, and beneficent presence of physician with patient—be it in-person or virtual—is immutable, woven as it always has been into the redemptive fabric of the created order. We must respond to our high calling to reclaim that good and healing presence for the good of every suffering, sacred person.[70]

69. Barry, *Great Influenza*, chap. 1.

70. I would like to thank Robert Cochran and Richard Campanelli for their excellent advice in preparing this manuscript.

Contributors

Denis Alexander is the founding director (emeritus) of the Faraday Institute for Science and Religion at the University of Cambridge, where he is emeritus fellow of St. Edmund's College.

Marcel Biato is a Brazilian amabassador to Ireland and the United Nations Commission of Nuclear Sources of Production.

Alberto R. Coll is Vincent de Paul Professor of Law and U.S. Foreign Relations at De Paul University College of Law. He was also principal deputy assistant secretary of defense for the Pentagon.

Anson Kung is a Canadian-born engineer and entrepreneur who founded A&K Robotics in 2015 and Oco Meals in 2020.

Mark Maxwell is president of Prairie College and president of Tower Asset Management.

John Purvis is a consultant on banking, finance, business development and former member of the European Parliament (1979–1984, 1999–2009).

Allen H. Roberts is associate medical director and professor of clinical medicine at Georgetown University Hospital.

Michael Tai is professor of international trade at the University of Cambridge.

Hon. Rollin A. Van Broekhoven is a retired federal judge for the US government.

CPSIA information can be obtained
at www.ICGtesting.com
Printed in the USA
BVHW081506090522
636461BV00004B/25